GUILTY WITHOUT TRIAL

GUILTY WITHOUT TRIAL
Women in the Sex Trade in Calcutta

Carolyn Sleightholme
and
Indrani Sinha

 Rutgers University Press
New Brunswick, New Jersey

First published in India 1996 by
STREE, 16 Southern Avenue, Calcutta 700 026

First published in the United States 1997 by
Rutgers University Press, New Brunswick, New Jersey

© 1996 STREE

Library of Congress Cataloging-in-Publication
Data is available upon request

ISBN 0-8135-2380-X (cloth)
ISBN 0-8135-2381-8 (pbk)

Typeset and design by Compuset International
85 Park St, Calcutta 700 016

... through midnight streets I hear
How the youthful harlot's curse
Blasts the newborn infant's tear
And blights with plagues the marriage hearse.

— William Blake

Contents

Foreword

MY JOURNEY, MEETING sex-workers and getting to hear their stories at first hand began in 1977. That was when I got to know Rupali and Sonali, two sex-workers of Sonagachhi. Soon I came in contact with twenty-three Nepalese child prostitutes who had been rescued from a red-light area and placed in a home run by the government. I realized that before I could offer effective help, I would have to understand the social system that permitted thousands of little girls to be brought to service the red-light areas of Calcutta, Bombay and Delhi. There were many hurdles on the way, and it was only in 1989 that a group of people who shared my concerns came together to form Sanlaap, and we began our work with sex-workers.

The world is very concerned over the issue of the neglected girl child. Let us look at a section of them whose lives seem particularly hopeless. We have learnt a great deal about what they are put through every day, and can do very little to stop it. I am talking about child sex-workers. We are in touch with hundreds of children, young girls and women who are slaves to the oldest profession in the world. We need to question the system that allows them to cross borders to reach the brothels of the big cities in our region. We need to find out how and why they return to the brothels after they have been 'rescued', after going through the due judicial process.

This book draws upon the experiences of all the staff and members of Sanlaap, a NGO (non-government organization) that we set up to work with sex-workers in the red-light areas. The path is untrodden and sometimes dangerous. It is the dedication and sincerity of the staff that has made this book possible. A book like this can never be complete because every day information keeps pointing to new developments. Even so, it will reveal the status of a community that is stigmatized and shunned by the society which has created it.

Because Sanlaap has worked with this community for a number of years, the government is considering giving us custody of rescued child sex-workers. We will be allowed access to the government remand home and will begin the major task of counselling and motivating them towards rehabilitation and a better future. Our long cherished dreams will therefore soon be realized. But our journey will still not be over.

I would like to thank the staff and members of Sanlaap and especially the people who continue to help us in our work in the red-light areas. I would also like to thank several of the organizations and individuals who helped us with their experience and shared information that has made this book possible. I would specially like to thank many senior members of the police, who are very supportive of our work.

Finally, all my thanks go to Carolyn who worked with dedication and sensitivity to put the many disparate strands into a book that we hope will be accessible to many people. We would also like to convey our appreciation to Stree, our publishers, who convinced us that our story must be told, and for their constant support and encouragement.

Calcutta 1996   I S

Preface

'If you see a woman who is always laughing, fond of gaming and jesting, always running to her neighbours, meddling with matters that are no concern of hers, plaguing her husband with constant complaints, leaguing herself with other women against him, playing the grand lady, accepting gifts from everybody, know that that woman is a whore without shame.'

—*The Perfumed Garden*

TO BE LABELLED a whore is intended as a great insult; to be labelled a whore without shame a greater insult still. What we have tried to show in this book is that the shameful face of the red-light areas is the moral, legal and social isolation of the residents. This is not the shame of the sex-workers, but the shame of the rest of society. Our own shame.

Non-governmental organizations (NGOs) have emerged as a significant interventionist force in Calcutta's red-light areas over the past few years. Sanlaap, founded in 1989, is among them. The origins of this book lie in a report documenting Sanlaap's experiences in the red-light areas. It gradually enlarged its focus to include a detailed account of the sex trade based upon the experiences of other local NGOs and a review of existing literature. The authors divided their responsibilities: Indrani Sinha, founder-member of Sanlaap, shared the

information and experiences of the organization she heads;
Carolyn Sleightholme carried out additional research, developed the analysis and wrote the text. The book reaches into
the women's lives to present a broad overview of the sex trade.

It is now being more widely recognized that the priorities
poor people set for themselves do not necessarily match with
the priorities set for them by policy-makers. The involvement
of beneficiaries in the decision-making process is now accepted
as crucial to the success of programmes that are tailor-made
for them. But how often do the governments or the NGOs take
the trouble to find out what the people themselves have identified and prioritized as their problems? Both the government
and the NGOs, being outsiders, frequently jump too quickly
into projects that are not need-based, which then reflect instead the interests and preoccupations of the outsiders themselves. The NGOs are expected to have a little more flexibility
and to be more in touch with the grass roots than governments. They are also supposed to be more participatory because of their size and autonomy. Yet many NGOs working
with sex-workers reflect the needs and interests of their middle class staff rather than those of the sex-workers themselves.
There is a world of possibilities for relevant and need-based
interventions over and above schools, creches and clinics for
sexually transmitted diseases (STDs). These interventions
could even promote the long-term strategic interests of the
sex-workers.

In this book we suggest a range of interventions which could
help to address both the short-term and long-term needs of the
Calcutta sex-workers. For example, we argue that income-generation projects with sex-workers reflect one of the prejudices
that pushes women into sex-work in the first place: the myth
that women only require 'pin money', a small income which
needs to be supplemented because it is not enough to raise a
family. Gender-stereotypical occupations such as sewing and
knitting do not provide a livelihood. Without skills which can
earn a woman enough to raise a family, a single woman or a female head of a household will have to continue in a profession
which is not of her choice and which cannot continue once she
grows old. Income-generation projects with sex-workers are not
necessarily clear about their objectives. Are they offering an al-

ternative livelihood or a few supplementary rupees? Are they trying to help women leave the profession because of the NGO staff's own moral viewpoint, or because the women themselves have expressed a desire to leave?

Today in Calcutta the practical needs of the sex-workers are gradually being brought into focus, although the spotlight is still overwhelmingly on sexual health as HIV-related funds pour in to control the epidemic. According to the 1995 data of the National Aids Control Organization (NACO), in India there have been 7.79 HIV cases per 1000 screened (see Chapter 4). It is to be hoped that this new interest in the sex trade can be harnessed to tackle wider issues of power between sex-workers and the organizers of the sex trade, pimps and clients, *babus* or lovers (long-term clients), and between sex-workers and society in general. We hope that the new focus on the sex industry will help to promote group formation among sex-workers as a means of minimizing inequalities, an objective which is fundamental to any far-reaching change in the interest of the sex-workers in particular, and of women in general. Already, concerns over the spread of HIV/AIDS have given the sex-workers a new bargaining power. Several leaders have sprung up from the red-light areas who are articulating their demands, taking independent initiatives and refusing to be silenced. There are a growing number of women who are holding their heads high and demanding rights for women in their profession—without shame.

Radical changes are not easy to envisage. They involve challenging overwhelmingly powerful and entrenched interests. We hope that the latent strength and largely dormant power of different sex-worker groups to organize, challenge and to mobilize can be activated; and that the sex-workers will rise up and sustain themselves without dependence on, but with the support of, mainstream organizations. We also hope that institutions of the state such as the law and the police will have the flexibility to change and to respond to pressures from the sex-workers; that a significant change in attitudes towards sexuality and women's need for economic independence will take place.

Our unwavering objectives are: (*i*) the elimination of forced prostitution; (*ii*) the elimination of exploitation and abuse of sex-workers; (*iii*) the support of sex-workers' demand for basic human rights; and (*iv*) the reduction of discrimination by gender. We have to remember that the plight of the sex-workers is strongly linked to the status of all women. In the words of the Filipina activist, Maria Castaneda:

> As long as a woman can be bought or sold,
> no woman is free.

Calcutta, 1996   C. S.

Acknowledgements

We are indebted to all of the women who shared their thoughts and experiences with us, and to the staff of Sanlaap who gave their time and support while the book was being written. Particular thanks are given to those friends and colleagues who read through drafts of the book and gave valuable comments, in particular to Catrin Evans for her painstaking efforts to overhaul the first draft, to Malika Singh for her fresh insights, and to Stree, our publishers, for their patience and support. Thanks also to our families for their tolerance.

GUILTY WITHOUT TRIAL

MAP: CALCUTTA AND ITS NEIGHBOURING AREAS

Introduction

PROSTITUTION IS OFTEN referred to as 'the oldest profession' and the working women are known as 'fallen women', 'public women', or are referred to in insulting and derogatory terms such as *randi* or *veshya*, similar in tone to the English word 'whore'. Although we choose to use the more respectful description 'sex-worker' which has fewer connotations than the word 'prostitute', there is no denying that she receives no respect whatsoever. Sex-workers are an outcaste group, rejected by mainstream society, hidden away in red-light areas. They are represented in popular Indian films and literature through stereotypes of 'bad' women.

WHY THIS BOOK?

This book aims to go beyond the stereotypes that shape our ideas of women who work as commercial sex-workers, presenting their lives and our experiences of working with them in order to influence attitudes, policies and practice. As practitioners we offer our understanding of the issues that we see as being central to the lives of sex-workers. This book is intended to be easily accessible to a wide range of readers, especially to researchers and practitioners in government and non-government organizations. We believe that more information and openness about the sex industry will create an understanding of sex-workers, not as criminals but as victims and survivors, victims and survivors of a society that creates prostitution. We must accept sex-workers not with pity or contempt but with respect as people with rights like ourselves.

If the experiences of sex-workers and of the NGOs who work with them are more fully understood by other practitioners and researchers, then a small step has been taken towards building an alternative. We hope that every reader will be a part of this change. We attempt to break the invisibility and isolation of sex-workers and generate more understanding. We have recommended strategies at the end of the book that we feel reflect the women's needs in the short term as well as address more strategic issues to increase gender equality in the long term.

WHY THE SEX TRADE EXISTS

Debates about why prostitution exists have generally focused on sex-workers either as deviants or as victims of poverty. Believing that sex-workers are social and psychological deviants is a justification for stigmatizing them as 'bad women' and absolving society of any responsibility or blame for their condition. This belief has no explanation for the sheer numbers of women who keep entering the profession, nor does it explore why the demand is there in the first place. It takes for granted that 'normal' men are polygamous by nature, while 'normal' women are monogamous.

Moreover, the belief that economic difficulties force women into the sex trade points to society's responsibility and acknowledges that the majority of the women are joining the trade as a survival strategy. This is only a partial explanation. Poverty alone cannot account for the gender dimension of the sex trade whereby women are providing the service and men are being serviced. Economic arguments rarely explore how people's needs are strongly influenced by their gender.

The Gender Perspective

The gender perspective of commercial sex is the one which is most frequently overlooked. Central to this perspective are the division of labour according to a person's gender, and society's *gender and poverty*

double standards of sexual morality. Indian society is patriarchal, characterized by male control over female labour and female sexuality, separating men and women into different domains where the world of women is under-valued and insecure. In extreme poverty or when crises occur in the family, women who have to support themselves and their families have limited resources to fall back on. Men are more likely to have access to resources through economically productive skills, existing jobs and income, land and housing, which are frequently not available to women in times of crisis such as desertion or widowhood. Poverty itself affects men and women differently, and women who have been dependent all their lives are more vulnerable and have fewer independent survival options than men. Women's labour is mostly restricted to the household, which is under male control, and when poverty forces them to work outside the household, they do so at a disadvantage to men. They have rarely been raised with appropriate skills, and face the additional burden of managing the home and the family as well as doing paid work simultaneously. Women's work is either underpaid or unpaid, as women are neither educated nor trained with a view to being economically independent. Women are structurally disadvantaged in the workforce. It is partially because of this unequal division of labour by gender that so many women join the sex trade when they have to start earning a livelihood.

A 'good' woman's domain is clearly the family and the home, and her status and security are based on her relationships to men, primarily to her husband. Within the family a woman is dependent and therefore has limited options for survival outside marriage and family. A woman's honour is strongly linked to her sexuality through chastity before marriage and faithfulness after, and she is severely punished if she deviates from this norm. A man's honour, however, is not linked to his sexuality in the same way, but to his behaviour in areas outside the family and the home. In Indian society contrary messages about sex are given out. On the one hand, media and popular culture increasingly display images of women as sexual commodities, as playthings for men's sexual desires; at the same time we teach women to reserve their bodies for marriage and for one man, and to be a modest wife and mother. A man's sexual behaviour can be expressed in various ways outside marriage, and married men who have sex with other women are tolerated and not punished in the same way as women are. Also, while men can 'get away' with sex before marriage, women's virginity is seen as an absolute necessity. By using the phrase 'double standard of sexual morality', we point out that in patriarchal societies morality has two genders. It is this double standard that explains the stigmatization of commercial sex-workers. 'Respectable' members of society turn their backs on the plight of sex-workers and the uncomfortable issues their existence raises.

Legal Approach

India's legal approach towards the sex industry upholds this double standard. Sex-workers are committing a crime if they are found to solicit or practise within or near a public place. They can be removed from any place at the request of a magistrate, they can lose their children, and they can be evicted at any time. The police haul off sex-workers periodically, keep them in a lock-up for a while before taking money from them and releasing them to continue their profession. Under the law the client, however, only commits a crime if he is practising with a sex-worker in a public place or is having sex with a girl under sixteen. The Sixty-Fourth Law Commission Report investigating prostitution laws argued against the punishment of male clients, quoting the following in support of its arguments:

> The professional prostitute, being a social outcaste, may periodically be punished without disturbing the usual course of society . . . the man, however, is something more than a partner in an immoral act; he discharges important social and business relations, is a father or brother responsible for the maintenance of others, has commercial or industrial duties to meet. He cannot be imprisoned without damaging society (Haksar and Singh 1992:68-69).

The fact that commercial sex-workers are also responsible for others, not least their children, was conveniently forgotten.

Debates about the future of the sex trade have focused on

its legal position. One argument is for the legalization of the profession as a means of regulating it and removing the criminal element, while the other is for attempting to abolish the sex trade by criminalizing it and rigorously enforcing the law. Those who are pro-legalization often argue that commercial sex-workers reduce the incidence of rape and make it possible for men who have no sexual partner, or who have different sexual preferences to those of their partners, to express their sexuality in a harmless way. Many sex-workers themselves use these arguments, pointing out that as their work serves a social purpose they should be free of police harassment and discrimination. Those who argue for the abolition of the sex trade focus on the negative effects by pointing out that the sex trade caters to and perpetuates the commodification of women, that it could actually increase abuse against women because it reinforces the attitude that women can be purchased and used by men. Legalizing it would legitimize the myth that men have an uncontrollable sex drive. These arguments are often used by feminists who are working to change society's attitudes to women and sexuality. Others, including some senior police officials, argue for abolishing the sex trade simply because it is 'immoral', and hope that they can stamp it out by using the law to disperse the red-light areas and impose state rehabilitation on the women.

We argue for an approach towards prostitution which sees gender inequalities as an important underlying cause along with economic inequalities. We believe in working towards a more gender-equal society in the long term so that more women will be economically independent, have more control over their sexuality, and their honour will not be judged on their sexual behaviour and their relationships with men. Because the nature of prostitution is a very complex one, we do not support the demand for abolition, as forcing through abolition without tackling the root causes would push the sex trade underground. We realize, however, that legalization may not lead to the destigmatization of the sex-worker. Legalization, without strong monitoring and regulation by the sex-workers and their supporters, may instead enable the state to interfere in their lives and subject them to further humiliation. Certainly, within the existing toleration laws, we would support the demand to repeal those clauses which criminalize the sex-workers and deny them their basic rights. We argue for the de-criminalization of soliciting, with the primary objective of reducing police harassment. We would also like to see the law allow for punishment of the client for non-payment or for refusing to wear a condom. These ideas are explored in detail in Chapter 4.

METHODOLOGY

We present case studies and share the field experiences of Sanlaap, a small non-government organization run by women. This book is not based on any specific research project but is a collection of information, stories and experiences. Individual case studies have been recorded in the course of our work that involves provision of child-care, health awareness, counselling and support to sex-workers. We have drawn primarily on our field experiences, and have included analysis of different survey results, information gained from a review of existing literature and from interviews with key people. In the case studies all names have been changed for the sake of anonymity but the information gathered remains intact. While sharing our experiences we acknowledge that our accounts are inevitably subjective. Most of the information we present is not accompanied by empirical evidence. We are aware of the limitations of this approach but also of the difficulties of gathering quantitative information in such a sensitive area and the danger of over-valuing the results once they have been turned into supposedly objective facts and figures.

To broaden our understanding of the commercial sex trade, we have covered issues which bring out the many dimensions of a sex-worker's life. The introduction begins with an overview of the red-light areas in Calcutta, the scale of the sex industry, and how the financial and living arrangements are organized. In Chapter 1 we explore why women enter the profession, and find that while financial problems are a constant factor, the actual events which finally push them into the trade are usually linked to women's insecurity and vulnerability within the family during times of crises. In Chapter 2 we focus on trafficking of women for money, how common this is and how it is organized both informally and formally. We show that trafficking of women to and from Calcutta's red-light areas is flourishing despite stringent anti-trafficking laws, and how Calcutta functions as both source and receiving areas, and a transit centre for trafficking of women and girls. In Chapter 3 we examine the prostitution laws in India, and show from women's own experiences how the laws are actually implemented on the ground. This reveals a depressing picture of police harassment, ignorance of the sex-worker and non-implementation of the special laws for trafficking.

In Chapter 4 we look into the health problems faced by sex-workers, broadly interpreting health to include violence and abuse. We find that sex-workers are relatively aware about sexually-transmitted diseases (STDs), including HIV/AIDS, but are often powerless to address them. Sex-workers also suffer from various other work-related and environment-related illnesses. Other general health issues and women's health problems are no less important but have been neglected by organizations working on health issues in red-light areas. In Chapter 5 we briefly look at the financial situation of female sex-workers in Calcutta, showing that the money earned is limited, short-lived and used to support many dependents, including families in the women's native villages. As compensation for the work and the lifestyle the financial rewards are indeed meagre. Chapter 6 presents the women as mothers and looks at the problems faced by them and their children, problems such as child-care, education and discrimination. Few sex-workers want their daughters to join the profession, and most do their utmost to educate them and rear them to have alternatives. Chapter 7 briefly discusses the relationships that clients have with the women, how these range from one-off to regular visits, to becoming live-in partners or husbands. Through clients, and the more long-term relationships with men known as *babus*, a range of different financial and living arrangements are available to sex-workers. In Chapter 8 we look at the kind of interventions that are being promoted by outsiders and the initiatives coming from within. Although there is a proliferation of NGO activity in the red-light areas as a result of growing concerns over the HIV/AIDS epidemic, few government or NGO interventions are finely tuned to the exact needs of the women, neither in the short term nor in the long term. In some of these areas strong female leaders have emerged and they are representing the felt needs of the women more accurately. We end by offering a few recommendations for practitioners and policy-makers.

As we are writing from our experiences of working in the red-light areas, we have been unable to include certain information. The experiences of the floating sex-workers, part-time women who return to families at the end of a day's work, are discussed briefly in the Introduction. What little information we have about male sex-workers catering to men who have sex with men is included in Appendix I to give a more complete picture of the commercial sex trade in Calcutta. Unfortunately we have no information about the higher class call girls who operate in Calcutta.

THE MARGINALIZATION OF WOMEN

The history of prostitution in India reveals that the common or 'street' prostitute has always existed alongside higher class courtesans. In ancient India, there were women skilled in music and dance who also provided sexual pleasure: there was the *devadasi*, or temple dancer, the *baiji*, or classical singer, and concubines in the royal courts. Compared to them the common or 'street' prostitute faced much more degradation and was more of an outcaste. The precarious situation of today's commercial sex-workers is a reflection of the further marginalization of women as a result of social and economic changes. For these women with limited or no options, joining the sex trade is a matter of survival (Joarder 1985).

The gradual marginalization of the cottage industries from the beginning of the nineteenth century onwards displaced many women from traditional employment. Until the 1881 Indian Factories Act, women and children were not allowed to enter the newly emerging industrial labour market; but even after this enactment, women found themselves in menial underpaid jobs. In the jute mills these women were referred to as 'sweepers' and regarded as part-time prostitutes (Chatterjee 1992: 25). The red-light area of Sonagachhi and its satellites,

Sett Bagan and Ram Bagan, were growing around this time to serve traders and male migrant labourers who flocked to Calcutta. Commercial sex was also in demand from British soldiers. Under British rule cantonment prostitutes were legally available for the use of soldiers. Brothels were licensed and abundant in the central areas of Calcutta (Joarder 1985). In 1879, 2,458 registered brothels were operating in Calcutta alone (Chatterjee 1992: 13-14). Many of the women who came into the sex trade in Calcutta at this time were destitute Hindu widows, lower caste women and children sold by their parents during times of famine. By 1911, nearly 25 percent of the working women in Calcutta were sex-workers. The actual figure recorded in the 1911 Census was 14,271, second only to 22,409 domestic servants.

By the early twentieth century Sonagachhi and Harkata Lane (near Bowbazar) were flourishing red-light areas. Harkata Lane served students of nearby colleges, including Hindu College. Sonagachhi was the home of upper class sex-workers, most of whom were kept by rich men, and who never solicited on the streets but worked through pimps. Bowbazar was also populated with high-class baijis. Sett Bagan was a more down-market area close to Sonagachhi, populated with women migrants from the rural areas. The red-light area at the docks in the Watgunj-Kidderpore area served sailors and traders. A written account of 1930 describes Watgunj as serving Japanese sailors; it mentions thirty-four Japanese sex-workers who wore traditional dress and lived in brothels decorated with Japanese lanterns (Joarder 1985: 70). The Diamond Harbour red-light area grew around the docks and also catered to the needs of the many male traders who came from the South 24-Parganas district. The Kalighat red-light area grew around the famous Kalighat Temple.[1] A number of *dharamshalas*, or rest houses where pilgrims, traders and travellers could stay, were established around the temple. Many young men who came from the villages stayed in these dharamshalas, and women from poor families were brought in to cook and clean for them. These same women also served them sexually. With time a commercial sex trade began to flourish in the area to serve pilgrims, traders and others.

THE SEX TRADE IN CALCUTTA

Calcutta's red-light areas are home to approximately 20,000 female commercial sex-workers plus their families.[2] The precise population of practising female commercial sex-workers in Calcutta is impossible to estimate as some women live in one red-light area but practise in another, and many part-time 'flying' or 'floating' sex-workers work in the red-light areas but return to their homes and families elsewhere at the end of the day. The estimated figure of over 20,000 includes only the female commercial sex-workers who both live and work in the red-light areas. The number of practising sex-workers is also subject to seasonal variation.

The scale of the industry is immense. If we estimate that these women see an average of three or four clients daily, then between 60,000 to 80,000 men are visiting commercial sex-workers in Calcutta every day. The All-India Institute of Hygiene and Public Health (AIIH&PH) estimates that 20,000 men visit the sex-workers in Sonagachhi alone (AIIH&PH 1995: 3). The high turnover of women in the sex industry means that hundreds of new girls are joining every year, while there are thousands of aged former sex-workers in the city. We also have to consider the many other people who benefit from the sex industry: the landlords and landladies (*bariwalas*, *malkins* or *mashis*—the latter is the kinship term for maternal aunt, though no such relationship actually exists), the pimps (*dadas*), live-in partners, regular clients or lovers (babus), trafficking agents, police, moneylenders.

The housing in the red-light areas is generally overcrowded, with whole families or several sex-workers living and working in the same room. Rooms are usually part of large houses which are rented out by single landlords and rent is usually paid on a daily basis, with extras for fans and TVs. Because there is little space many women cook in the corridors or on the steps outside their rooms, and use high beds that provide space underneath for utensils and sleeping children. Toilet and bathing facilities are shared among many households, and water is collected from handpumps. In a survey conducted by AIIH&PH in 1993 (Singh 1995: 1), 15.6 percent of sex-workers were found to be literate.

Sex-workers in Calcutta either work independently or live and/or work under the *aadhiya* or *chukri* systems. Women working independently are frequently those who have left other areas after having worked in the chukri system, almost like bonded labourers. Now they simply rent a room on a daily, weekly or monthly basis, solicit clients for themselves, and keep all of their income with which they pay rent, bribes and other expenditures. In Kalighat the majority of the women work independently.

Under the aadhiya system several women use one room and give 50 percent of their earnings from each client to the mashi, who may own the room or may herself be a tenant. (The rate is actually 50 percent plus one rupee: so the owner of the room is always slightly better off in the deal.) Out of the remaining 50 percent the sex-worker pays for her own food, clothes, and other personal expenses, and often supports other family members. The aadhiya system is most common in the Sonagachhi, Kidderpore and Bowbazar areas of Calcutta, as well as in individual houses in other areas. The mashis are usually former sex workers. Often many women are working in one room that a queuing system operates for the beds during busy hours.

Many of the women who work in the aadhiya system are part-time 'flying' or 'floating' sex-workers. These women work in the red-light areas during the day but return to their own homes and families at night. Some floating sex-workers do actually live in a different red-light area but do not practise there. Either they can make more money in another area and are harassed less by the police, or they do not want to attend to clients with their children around. Most floating sex-workers live in ordinary family homes and are working as sex-workers to supplement or provide a family income. AIIH&PH estimates that 1,500 floating sex-workers visit Sonagachhi (Singh 1995: 3).

As a group floating sex-workers are quite vulnerable because they are not part of the red-light area community . Some facilities and security are available for women who live and work in these areas: for example, moneylenders are easily available in the red-light areas; if residential sex-workers are arrested they will be quickly bailed out by their mashis; older sex-workers are available to help with child-care; being known in the area also protects the fixed sex-workers from violence from clients as neighbours and acquaintances are more likely to intervene. In areas where women's groups have emerged, women who live in the area have an opportunity to be members, or at least they are known to local groups or clubs. Non-residential floating sex-workers, on the other hand, operate alone, isolated, and without this community support. Unfortunately we have hardly any contact with, or information about, the floating sex-workers. There is an urgent need for greater understanding of their lifestyles, and consequently what support they might need both at home and at work. Most of the women who work in the public places around central Calcutta are floating sex-workers.

Under the chukri system which is found in the Kidderpore-Watgunj area, the sex-worker, as mentioned earlier, is like a bonded labourer. Women sold into the chukri system are actually kept in sexual slavery. New sex-workers are totally controlled by a mashi or a dada who takes all their earnings until such time as they have repaid their debt, that is, their purchasing price plus any other expenses incurred during their time as chukri. The mashis or pimps pay for all expenses during this time, including food, clothes, health care and bribes to the police, but every rupee spent accumulates as the sex-worker's debt. In reality a sex-worker working in the chukri system will have repaid her debt at least twice before she is free to leave, at which point the mashi and clients are anyway ready for a new and younger face. When the women finally leave they usually start operating independently elsewhere in the city. In the aadhiya system the mashis are still important decision-makers; they may take on the role of moneylenders and exercise limited control over the women who work in their rooms. The aadhiya sex-workers are relatively free, in comparison with those under the chukri system, from the overwhelming influence of the mashi.

The lives of the sex-workers are influenced a great deal by local power groups which in Calcutta centre around clubs formed in allegiance with political parties. Youth clubs are small community organizations run by and for men. Often several clubs will cover the same geographical area but will usually draw their membership according to party affiliations.

Clubs are involved in direct political work such as organizing campaigns, protests and manipulating votes during elections, but are also an important social base as they organize sports, social events and other community activities. Some clubs have a social welfare orientation and work with the NGOs and other outside groups. Although women are rarely members, they are expected to participate in functions and are frequently forced to attend political rallies and give donations. Due to their political connections and their group strength, the club boys are often responsible for the law and order situation of a particular area. Young men from the red-light areas have little chance of finding stable employment and channel a lot of their energies into the work of the clubs, often linked to organizing the sex trade. Local *goondas* or hoodlums are often associated with a particular club and a political party.

Many sex-workers have clients who visit them regularly and pay them a fixed monthly sum. When a man becomes more than just a client he is referred to as the babu, which implies a relationship that goes beyond sex. A woman may have several babus. Some babus live with the women and are financially dependent on them, although even when such role reversals occur, both women and men tend to behave like traditional couples, with the men as the main decision-makers and the women continuing to manage the household and childcare, even tolerating domestic violence. Most women do aspire to have a long-term relationship with one man, and the concept of 'mental monogamy' does exist even though the women may be having other sexual relationships for money. Many women believe that they will only become pregnant if they love their sexual partner and that their children are fathered by their babus and not their clients.

The nature of the sex trade today is purely commercial. In popular culture, Hindi films occasionally take us back to the days of the nineteenth-century courtesans with their upper class clients, but more often than not they remind us that the prostitute is an outcaste, to be lusted after by men but always rejected in favour of the chaste and honourable woman. The truth is a far cry from the stereotype of the prostitute. She is also an honourable woman: mother, head of a household, breadwinner of a family, often supporting other elderly and vulnerable members. If we put the whole contradictory issue of sex and sexuality aside for a moment, and look at honour as the dignity of work, of diligence, of rising above adversity and developing a survival strategy which is harmless to others, then we begin to see how honour can be applied to the commercial sex-worker, and how dishonour can be applied to the person who discredits and marginalizes her.

NOTES

1. The Kalighat Temple is an important pilgrimage site in south Calcutta. It is dedicated to the Goddess Kali.
2. We estimate that around 7,500 sex-workers work in Sonagachhi, and satellite areas, 1,500 in Bowbazar, 500 in Kalighat, 150 in Amtala, 100 in Diamond Harbour. In addition to these red-light areas which are known to us, around 7,000 are in the huge Watgunj-Kidderpore area, and considerable numbers work in Loker Math, Sett Bagan, Ram Bagan, Tollygunge, Chetla and many other areas in Calcutta and Howrah, giving an approximate total of 20,000.

CHAPTER 1

A Strategy for Survival

W HAT COMPELS WOMEN to enter the sex trade? Poverty is
undoubtedly the overriding factor, and it affects men and
women differently. By looking at physical and sexual abuse,
child marriage, desertion and widowhood, we discover that the
position of women is as crucial a factor as their financial as-
sets. It is these two factors, along with contact with the sex
trade, either directly or through agents, that combine to push
women into sex-work.

SURVEY FINDINGS

In Calcutta, the majority of women have entered the profession
for their own or their family's survival. Women resort to it as
a survival strategy when poverty has thrust financial responsibility onto their shoulders. Most women cite poverty as the
single most important factor compelling them to join the profession, needing to support themselves, their families and their
children. A high number say they were betrayed by people who
offered them jobs, or were persuaded by people they knew—
friends or family. In a survey conducted by Sanlaap (1994, unpublished), we asked 257 sex-workers the main reason why
they joined the profession, and received the following responses
(Table 1.1):

TABLE 1.1 Reasons for Becoming Sex-Workers

Economic difficulties	52
Violence from husband	28
Family problems	24
Cheated or misled	13
Came with husband/lover	11
Widowed	11
Divorced or deserted	10
Chose to come	10
Sold	9
Brought by friend/relative	9
Mother's profession	6
Orphaned	6
Violence from in-laws	5
Born in a red-light area	3
Child marriage	2
To escape destitution after riot	2
No answer	56
Total	257

Source: Sanlaap survey, 1994

Although the responses to this question state only the main reason and do not mention other social and economic circumstances at the time of joining, despite being an over-simplification, they do give an indication of the relevant factors. What emerges is how many family and marriage break-ups compel women to join the sex trade. A similar survey of 450 women in Sonagachhi, conducted by the AIIH&PH (Singh 1995: 7), found that 49.1 percent mentioned acute poverty, 21.56 percent a family dispute, 15.56 percent said they were misled, 8.67 percent said they came willingly, 4.67 percent mentioned family tradition and 0.44 percent said they were kidnapped.

Poverty and Migration

Calcutta is the major city of eastern India and historically has absorbed migrants and refugees from its neighbouring states as well as from Nepal and Bangladesh.[1] Not only is the city itself a site of widescale poverty, but its vast hinterland and the area across the country's eastern and northern borders also contains millions who live below the poverty line, and from where thousands of migrants flock to Calcutta every year (see Map). In the Sanlaap survey we found that 70 percent of the sex-workers we are involved with are from West Bengal. Of these, almost 30 percent are from Murshidabad district alone. Another 30 percent are from outside West Bengal, and 15 percent are from Bangladesh.

After the 1947 partition of India and the formation of East and West Pakistan and again after the 1970-71 Bangladesh war, a large number of Bangladeshis came to Calcutta as refugees.[2] The planned rehabilitation of these refugees was largely ineffective and so displaced communities have managed to fend for themselves, developing their own survival strategies. Even today Bangladesh remains one of the poorest countries in the world. Unofficial migration continues across the border, which is easy to cross without papers. West Bengal itself is bordered by Orissa and Bihar, and Madhya Pradesh is comparatively near. A large percentage of people here are extremely deprived and there is high outmigration. For example, in 1991, 40.8 percent of the population of Bihar was living below the poverty line. Bihar has been the poorest state in the country since pre-Independence and continues to hold this dubious distinction. Female literacy rates in neighbouring states, indicating the vulnerability of women, are all appallingly low, the highest being 34 percent in Orissa (Census 1991).

The economy of West Bengal has been in sharp decline since Independence. At the same time, the population has continued to grow, increasing by almost 25 percent in the decade 1981 to 1991. Calcutta bears the brunt of this economic decline. At present estimates one million of Calcutta's population live in slums (Census 1991), while there are between 75,000 to 100,000 street children in Calcutta (National Labour Institute 1991). The majority of the migrants to West Bengal have been men who have found employment in industry, while women predominate in the informal sector, working in small industries or as domestic workers. After Independence, because of the high number of migrant male workers, the sex ratio in Calcutta was 580 women for every 1,000 men. It has been rising since but is still low at 799 women for every 1,000 men, and 917 women for every 1,000 men for the whole of West Bengal (Census 1951; 1991).[3] There has thus been both a shortage of work for women, coupled with a high number of single men, creating a demand for sex-workers.

Until the seventies, domestic work and sex-work were two of the main employment options open to women. Nowadays more options do exist, although these are mostly in the unorganized sector. Increasing male unemployment and rural poverty have resulted in more women migrants coming to Calcutta in search of work, even though the reality of the work that is available leaves much to be desired. Many migrants are brought to Calcutta as temporary labour. Calcutta's workforce is highly politicized and unionized compared to other states, and some employers prefer to hire non-unionized labour from rural areas and neighbouring states. These labourers are given temporary work and shelter in temporary slums. At the end of their period of work they are expected to return to their villages but after experiencing a regular wage, many decide to stay on rather than return to the poverty of their villages. Finding new work and new shelter is not easy and eventually economic pressures become too much for some who end up joining the sex trade.

Let us hear the story of Kalpana, age 28:

> My mother was a widow in Bangladesh. She arranged my marriage when I was a child, and married me to a small-time businessman. Although he was quite successful in his work, Hindu-Muslim tensions in the area affected his business and the money stopped coming in. Eventually we decided to leave the village and cross over to India in search of work. My husband suggested we cross separately as we were going illegally, and one person would be less conspicuous than two. After crossing by myself I could not find my husband at the arranged meeting place. I don't know if my husband planned this. I spent several days searching for him. I was young, and people looked at me in a bad way when I searched or asked for refuge. One day I was approached by an old woman who befriended me and gave me shelter in the border area. This woman persuaded me to give up the search and go to Calcutta to find work—I even thought I might find my husband there.

She escorted me to Sonagachhi where I found lines of girls
and women of all ages standing on the streets, over made-
up and wearing indecent clothes. The old woman took me
to a small room where another lady gave me food, and
then I just fell asleep on a mat on the floor. I soon realized
what I would have to do.

All these stories end in the same way. Mornings bring sur-
prise; soon they understand what is to happen and either they
give in quietly, or else they are first forced into sexual intercourse by a client, a local thug or a pimp. Kalpana is now an
experienced sex-worker. She earns around Rs.150-200 per
day.[4] Nowadays she saves some money, despite paying half of
what she earns to her mashi. She spends lavishly on food.
Although she has visited her village in Bangladesh twice since
coming to India, she did not find her husband, and nobody
knows where he is. After each visit she returns to Calcutta.
Nobody is going to look after her back in her village. 'In some
ways I am better off than before because these days I eat well.
But I have become "bad", and there is no going back.'

Then there is the example of Munawar. As a housewife
she had lived in the South 24-Parganas district of West
Bengal, and had given birth to four children by the time
she was twenty-two, when her husband left her to marry
a second time. She continued to live with her parents-in-law
in a small room of her own. Slowly she sold off whatever
valuables she had, waiting for her husband to return to her
and the children. Eventually she gave up hope. When she
was told by her parents-in-law that they could not feed her
and her children any longer, she left the village and came
to Calcutta in search of work.

Munawar joined her mother who sold utensils in exchange
for old clothes, going from house to house. She lived in a slum
room with her parents, just managing to feed her children
who spent most of their time out on the pavement because
there was just not enough space for them all. She first entered
a red-light area while going from house to house selling utensils. She met and talked to women who had experienced similar hardships that she was now undergoing and who were now
earning far more than her. She talked to them about their
work. It took Munawar months to decide. Eventually she took

a room in a small red-light area, and shifted there with her children. It took away her *ijjat* (honour), she says, but provided her and her family with food and shelter. With the money she has saved she has managed to release a piece of land in her village that was lying with the moneylenders. Her son is now earning by working in a local garage, and she has one of her daughters in a hostel. She plans to return to the village one day, but this will only be possible if she manages to keep her life in Calcutta a secret.

Women Workers

It is a myth that women do not have to take on financial responsibilities. Statistics have shown that over a third of the world's households are headed by women who are solely responsible for all the household production and needs.[5] Women from refugee families, often originally from middle class Bengali households before displacement, may have been the first generation of female paid workers in their families, as traditional restrictions on women's employment outside the home quickly fell away when economic survival became a priority and overrode status considerations of keeping women as unpaid workers in the home. Alternatively, poor and lower caste families are more likely to have a tradition of female employment which sex-work is merely continuing. A study by Development Dialogue, a NGO that is based in Calcutta, found that a sex-worker in Calcutta sent an average of Rs.475 per month to families in rural areas (Das Gupta 1990: 10). These households may not even know that the earnings are coming from the sex trade.

Sita, rather than her brother, was the one who ended up supporting their mother. When Sita's marriage had broken down she returned to her natal home to live with her widowed mother and brother. Her mother was blind but her brother refused to support her, and so Sita decided to take her on as her own responsibility. They were living in Murshidabad which has strong links with the sex trade. Unable to find work anywhere else, she eventually came to Calcutta where she rented a room for her mother and herself and started work as a sex-worker. She hardly gets any clients now as she herself is growing old, so she has taken in two girls from Murshidabad who work in one of her rooms and give her half of their earnings under the aadhiya system. She earns about Rs.200 a day now as a mashi.

In some communities it has become socially acceptable for daughters to join the sex industry in order to support the family. The only group to study a source area in this region was Development Dialogue (Das Gupta 1990: 11) which went to the Rarh region of West Bengal—Barddhaman, Birbhum, Purulia, Bankura, north Midnapore—and found that 70 percent of the women in Calcutta brothels who had come from Murshidabad or Birbhum had actually come originally from this vast region. They found many women who joined prostitution as a traditional occupation because prostitution had been in the family for several generations. These women were not stigmatized and were welcomed back into their community during festivals and vacations. Many women were from landless families, many were destitute child brides or daughters from female-headed households. Families which were impoverished because their traditional caste occupation had died out were also sending girls into the sex trade. The main occupation of the area was agriculture, but women were not accustomed to, nor socially acceptable as agricultural labour. General trends in impoverishment and increasing landlessness affect male unemployment and disturb traditional livelihoods and so more and more women need to contribute to the family earnings.

Among the sex-workers in Calcutta, a majority support their own families rather than the families they are connected to through marriage. For example, Jatinder comes from a family of three sisters in Arambagh. The eldest sister was encouraged to become a sex-worker in Calcutta to support the whole family. When Jatinder first went to visit her sister she was disturbed by her work and tried to persuade her to leave. But she knew how much her family depended on her income as her parents were growing old and they were landless, without other earning members. Eventually, Jatinder went to live with her sister and then she too ended up earning for the family. Her sister tried to prevent her but Jatinder did not pay heed. She is now working in the sex trade alongside her sister. Between them they send money regularly back to their parents.

Deserted Single Women

Women have to stand on their own when their marriages fail. At the time of a wedding the whole community comes together to share in the celebration. If, later, the marriage experiences problems certain senior family and community members will try to help in bringing about a reconciliation. But if a reconciliation fails, the husband still has his place in the family; it is the wife who has to find a new home. There is no community support for her if her parents are old, if she has no way of earning a living, if she has to manage independently. She does this alone. Families who pay dowry for their daughters' marriages do not expect them to return later as dependents. There is a lot of social pressure on the women to reconcile with their husbands, however good or bad they may be. Women from broken marriages are at the mercy of the individual compassion of their parents to take them back and support them financially.

We remember Mita who was ill-treated by her husband during her first pregnancy. He wanted her to get rid of the baby but she refused to have an abortion. Her husband deserted her after the birth of their baby girl. She remained with her parents-in-law for a few days, but they refused even to give her food, so she returned to her parents. Her parents said they would not accept her back as her home was now with her parents-in-law. So when an old man approached her and offered her a job, she went along with him to Calcutta. As they reached the area that would become her home she realized what the nature of the work was and that she had no other choice but to overcome all her resistance and work in the sex industry. She tells us she wants to leave the profession but first and foremost would have to pay off a loan she took from a moneylender to cover the medical expenses for her daughter.

Widows

The 1991 Census found that there are 33 million widows in India, that is, 8 percent of the total female population of the country. The common belief that India's joint family system provides support to widows is a myth. A recent study by Marty

Chen of the Harvard Institute for International Development found that 62 percent of widows surveyed were living on their own with no support from families, and only 26 percent were found to be living in households headed by their sons (Chen, unpublished). Widows throughout India, primarily Hindus, upper and middle castes, are still not expected to re-marry. They have to lead very careful, restricted lives and any slight deviations lead to accusations of 'loose' behaviour. They are inauspicious, and are not even invited to community functions. Widows are legally entitled to a pension, maintenance from fathers-in-law, and land and property rights, although in practice these rights are rarely granted.

Young women are dependent on their fathers, and are raised to be dependent on their husbands. As old women they expect to be dependent on their sons. For some women this is unproblematic, while others discover the hidden dangers at their peril. If a woman has no sons, if she has an unfaithful, violent or ill husband, then the woman's security falls into someone else's hands and her dependency renders her powerless. Widows, in particular, fall foul of the dependency this society creates for women. If not granted the charity of parents-in-law or parents, a widow suddenly has to fend for herself despite never having been prepared for independence. Some of the widows inevitably end up working in the sex trade.

Munni is a twenty-four-year-old widow from Bihar who has a nine-year-old daughter. Less than a year after her husband's death her parents-in-law threw her and all her belongings out of the house. She left with her daughter and found a live-in job as a maid. She was very happy with the work because she was given food and shelter and her daughter was well looked after. Although the woman she worked for was very kind, her husband found Munni attractive and began making advances at her. She submitted to these advances because she was afraid of losing her job, and for months the man continued to use her for sex. One day his wife discovered what was going on and threw Munni out of the house. She survived by begging on the streets until a woman approached her and brought her and her daughter to a red-light area. She was soon initiated into the sex industry but managed to keep her daughter out

of it. From her earnings of approximately Rs.50 to 70 a day
she now pays room rent of Rs.15 per day, employs an *ayah*
or child-minder to look after her daughter in the evenings
while she works, and pays policemen whenever they come to
harass her. On top of her worries she has to suffer a landlord
who is violent and who now also abuses her sexually.

Child Marriage

Anu was married in Murshidabad at the age of eight. When
she was twelve years old her husband took a second wife and
Anu left his house. She went to her mother, who was a widow
living on the charity of her sons. Her sons were not willing to
take the responsibility for Anu and so her mother could do
nothing for her. Anu knew a woman who was working as a
sex-worker in a Calcutta red-light area. She went to stay with
her, and was given some work fetching and carrying things
for her friend's babu. But all she was getting paid was a couple
of rupees here and there, and she eventually ended up as a
sex-worker herself. She now earns Rs.100 a day and sends
money to her mother. Her mother is not aware of the nature
of her profession.

Over twenty-five million girls and ten million boys between
the ages of ten to fourteen are married in India (Census 1981).
At a young age the girls leave their families and have to cope
with many new experiences without support from known people. Child brides are usually from poor families who have married their daughters early because they cannot afford to keep
them. Sex can be very painful and traumatic for young and
undeveloped girls. Over two hundred and fifty thousand girls
in the above age group are divorced, widowed or separated,
as are over one hundred thousand of the boys. We know of at
least thirty cases of child brides who fled from their husbands
and who, unable to survive on their own, fell into the hands
of agents or pimps.

Let us consider what happened to Mina, for example. She
comes from a working class family in a Howrah village. She
has seven sisters. Her two elder sisters were married very
young, and much of the responsibility of the family fell on
Mina. By the age of twelve she was so frustrated with the

drudgery of endless housework and looking after her sisters that she readily agreed to marry a much older man when her parents arranged a match for her. Life with her new husband was very violent: he used her for sex at any time of the day and was very rough with her small body. At the age of thirteen she was not physically or emotionally prepared for this. In her misery she was befriended by a young man whose company she enjoyed and she began to sleep with him. Even then she did not enjoy sex, but she wanted his friendship. One day her husband beat her up very badly so she ran away to this man who took her to his friend's house in Calcutta. Initially he would visit her but after a few months his visits ceased. Then she was raped by his friend. She was fourteen years old. She ran away to Howrah Station where many young girls like her are sexually abused and eventually brought into the sex trade. The police saved her from the next logical step—she was sent to a government home and found to be pregnant.

Incest, Physical and Sexual Abuse

Durga was newly married when she learnt that her husband was an alcoholic. He used to lose control of himself and beat her up whenever he was drunk. Although she tried to tolerate his behaviour, one day he brought home a second wife and threw her out of the house. She would have accepted the situation because she had no other options. But she knew that her husband did not want her around and would do anything to get rid of her. She fled to her parent's house and took shelter there for some time, but all along she knew she was a burden on them and would eventually have to support herself financially. She had heard of an old woman who would be able to give her some work in Calcutta, so she came with her only to find herself sold into a brothel. She says that even if she had been able to escape, she would have nowhere else to go as she could not face her parents again.

The Sanlaap survey found that 13 percent of the sex-workers had joined the sex trade after leaving or being abandoned by violent husbands—who would beat them and also abuse them sexually—or by parents-in-law who would connive at their forced departures. While domestic violence occurs in homes of any class background, victims who end up in the sex industry are those who have no other resources to fall back on when they need security and shelter outside their marriages.

Chandra and her sister Suraj were both raped by their father at the ages of thirteen and fourteen. Suraj ran away from home and has not been seen by her family since. Chandra remained at home. When she finally summoned up the courage to tell her mother what had happened, her mother could do nothing to stop the situation and even started beating her up and taking it out on her. Her father raped her again and continued to abuse her whenever her mother was out of the house. At the age of sixteen she was married off to a man who kept her with him in a small room in a slum until he tired of her. Then he sold her to a red-light area. She managed to escape and now works independently as a sex-worker elsewhere. A hardened eighteen year old, resigned to her fate, she says, 'I should have charged my father also.'

Talking about and confronting incest is still taboo in India, and victims nurse their wounds in silence, often running away from home rather than admitting to anyone what has been happening. Sexual abuse outside the home is slightly more public, but remains largely underestimated as most victims still suffer in silence. A Sanlaap study among working women found a high number of cases of sexual abuse. Ayahs and housemaids are frequently abused by male employers when alone in the house. Vegetable vendors and petty traders are sexually harassed by railway police when travelling, by local hoodlums who control selling space on the streets, and by police when sleeping on the pavement before beginning early morning trading. Female pavement dwellers are especially vulnerable at night to rape (Sinha 1992). A study by CINI showed that approximately 90 percent of girls and 25 percent of boys living at Calcutta's Sealdah Station are sexually abused and raped by older children, local hoodlums and men from outside who visit the station (CINI 1992, reported in *Indian Express*, 6 April 1992). Girls are forcefully taken to parked railway carriages or raped on the platform and then given a small amount of money. This is their introduction to the world of commercial sex.

Indian society places so much importance on women's purity

and virginity that rape victims are instantly labelled 'damaged goods'. Rape victims have to cope not only with the trauma of the rape itself, but also with rejection by all who have a stake in their purity. Sometimes families of rape victims who are also very poor are afraid that their daughters are no longer marriageable and turn them out of the house. A large number of the girls living in Calcutta's welfare homes have been rejected by their parents after having been raped. Girls in this predicament have less to lose than others when joining the sex industry because they have already been labelled as 'whores'.

Seema comes from Midnapore where both her parents worked long hours in a nearby factory. During her adolescence she was alone every day except for the company of her elderly grandmother who would prepare her food. She started to idle her time away outdoors where men began to approach her. At the age of twelve she was molested by one of these men, who later gave her money and gifts. She did not confide in anyone. She did not understand what they were doing to her until one day at the age of fourteen she was raped. She tried to tell her parents but they would not listen, and she continued being used in this way, not knowing what else to do. The hoodlums who were abusing her started to arrange for other men to have sex with her, and they would take a cut of the money. This way she started operating as a 'flying prostitute', secretly practising by day and returning to her home at night. She was caught by the police one day and is now being treated for sexually transmitted diseases in a government remand home. It is not difficult to imagine the life ahead of her once she is released from the home.

Daughters of Sex-Workers

Children of sex-workers face particular problems integrating into the mainstream society. Stigmatized at school and reared in a home environment that is not conducive to formal learning and homework schedules, many drop out of school without qualifications. In Calcutta, even educated youths find it hard to get work; it is a generation that is either unemployed or largely underemployed. Children tainted with the background of having come from a red-light area find it especially difficult in the face of people's prejudices. Mothers who are sex-workers are usually very keen to get their daughters married off early so that they can leave the red-light area rather than live there during a vulnerable age. We hardly know of any daughters of sex-workers who were not married off at a young age. It is assumed by many people that most daughters of sex-workers join their mother's trade; this is, however, not the case.

The Sanlaap survey found that only 6 out of 257 practising sex-workers were daughters of sex-workers. For these few women, however, commercial sex-work has always been an option, following in their mother's footsteps. Brought up in the red-light areas, they have been exposed to sex at an early age, to sex as a commodity. They are familiar with the red-light areas, and know how the system works because they have links with the mashis and clients. It is easy for them to get accommodation in the area. They are much more down to earth about the profession than most outsiders who have never had day-to-day contact with it. And, besides, daughters of sex-workers are more realistic than other girls about how few women actually end up getting married and living happily ever after. Most have not experienced a family life with a steady and dependable father who supports the family. They are brought up in female-headed households, exposed to women who are the breadwinners, to men who come and go in fluid relationships, contributing little. They also know how hard it is for them to be accepted by mainstream society.

The daughters who do end up continuing their mother's profession do not usually join immediately but after a failed marriage or out of financial need later on in life. Mothers are usually very keen to set their daughters on a path that will lead them away from commercial sex. Many sex-workers send their children to schools which can keep them as boarders or to live with relatives in the rural areas. They try to keep them away from the influences of the red-light areas, especially from the sexual abuse which can be a cruel initiation into the world of prostitution.

Sharmila grew up in the one room where her mother practises as a sex-worker. She describes her experiences:

As a child I knew about my mother's activities. I remember a customer who used to beat my mother after his time with her. My mother never cried. I used to cry. One day I ran into the room and scratched him on the face. My mother beat me, afraid that the man would leave without paying. But he just laughed and dragged me into the bed. Later, he beat me out of the room. My first initiation had no ceremony. I just began one fine morning.

Many homes and institutions are unwilling to take in the children of sex-workers. For example, in 1932 the All Bengal Women's Union (ABWU) set up a home in Calcutta for 'rescued' sex-workers and their children. They actively campaigned for effective laws to combat trafficking. Later they took larger premises, accepted women referred to them by the government, and gradually the residents who had come from the sex industry became a minority. They were teased and maltreated by other residents. As the leadership in the organization changed, a more 'welfarist' approach began to take over and destitute women were given priority over sex-workers. The links with the sex industry came to be resented; for example, the people running the home disliked the visitors who came to see the children of sex-workers. Today, the ABWU admits they are reluctant to take sex-workers or their children into their homes because of the problems they have faced integrating them with the other residents.

Some NGOs do run homes specifically for the children of sex-workers and these, as well as hostel accommodation, are in great demand by mothers who want their children to grow up away from the red-light areas. The children in these homes do go on to join different professions, which serves as an effective counter to the prevailing prejudice.

A few sex-workers do want their daughters to go into the sex industry as they will be able to look after their mothers in their old age who usually have no other support; unlike other professions, the earning power of sex-workers decreases rather than increases with experience. Some daughters are initiated into the sex industry for other reasons but try to find ways out. The most obvious route is through marriage but this does not always work out as planned.

Gita was a young girl who wanted to see the world outside the red-light area where she had been brought up. She met a young man and they ran away together. Her mother, left alone, felt deserted as she had tried to bring her daughter up well and had expected her to stay on with her. She managed to find Gita and bring her back, persuading her to start practising as a sex-worker. Gita is now nineteen, still practising, and is already a mother of two children. She supports her mother who in turn looks after her children for her while she works.

Praveen's mother is also a former sex-worker who now runs an aadhiya business in one of the red-light areas. Praveen's first customer was a policeman from Lalbazar who said he would give her brother a job if she slept with him. This was her initiation (her brother was never given a job). She moved to another area and started practising there, but tried to think of a way out. In her new home she met a man who had a steady income. They had a good relationship but split up after a misunderstanding and she soon married another man who worked in a movie theatre. This man ill-treated her and forced her to continue in the profession, against her will. She began to see her old boyfriend again and finally ran away with him to her mother's place. They can manage without her income because her boyfriend has a good job, and she has been able to give up sex-work. She has three children now, one daughter is married and the youngest is in a boarding school. She works for a social welfare organization.

GENDER AND POVERTY

These stories reveal how limited the options are for unskilled women who find themselves, for one reason or another, in financial difficulties and without access to any economically secure household. These women are either members of a poor household, or have been separated from a household for some of the reasons mentioned earlier. Despite the myth that the men of the family are solely responsible for earning and supporting the family, in reality the burden also falls on the women. Yet women are not socially prepared for this role and are at a disadvantage when they have to take it on. They do not have any productive resources to fall back upon. *Streedhan* or jewellery gifted by a woman's parents at the time of her marriage can never be used to support a family, unlike land, which is in the hands of men.[6] Legally, women have rights to a share of parental property or that of their husbands', be it a house or a piece of land. In practice, more often than not, they do not get to benefit from it. Women are even prevented from doing certain types of agricultural labour and so they are excluded from a lot of the paid work which is available in rural areas. Without land, education, or skills for earning a living, women who have to support themselves and their families experience this struggle differently from men. They are dependent on the goodwill of relatives or their parents-in-law to support them, but even this is insecure and can be withdrawn at any time. When a woman tries to earn an independent income she may be treated with suspicion and be looked upon as a sex object. Without a husband, widows, single or separated women are seen as easy game for other men because they are not the 'property' of any particular man. Thus, they are prey to sexual harassment and exploitation.

Women therefore experience poverty and the struggle for survival differently from men. The possibilities open to women are both limited and insecure. Becoming a sex-worker is an obvious option if they are in contact with others who are already practising, or if they meet up with agents. Some women have suffered from sexual abuse and discover that taking money for sex is only a small step. These women have made rational decisions as coping or survival strategies, given their limited opportunities.

At some point in their lives most sex-workers have faced a crisis, social or economic, which has compelled them to leave their 'normal' life and join the sex trade, struggling to survive and rear their families, support their own parents or children, and take on the role of breadwinner with as much dignity as they can. It is not a matter of choice but of compulsion, of being compelled to become a sex-worker as a survival strategy, and then of learning to cope with this situation. Despite the low status of their work and the inherent sexual exploitation, women who work in the sex trade do not want to be treated as victims who deserve pity, any more than they want to be stigmatized and cast out. They are well aware that they deserve to be treated not as victims but as survivors.

NOTES

1. The estimated percentage of migrants in the total Calcutta population peaked at 56.2 percent in 1951 and has been decreasing since. The 1991 Census gives the most recent figure of 31.3 percent.
2. According to the figures provided by the Census of India, in the decade after Independence, 1951-1961, the population grew by 32.8 percent as opposed to 13.22 percent of the previous decade.
3. The lowest sex ratio for Calcutta was recorded in 1941 when there were 456 women for every 1,000 men. These figures can largely be explained by the male migrants who came into the city and did not bring their families.
4. The current exchange rate is around $1 = Rs 35. However, converting Indian incomes to dollars using this exchange rate can give a misleading picture. Prices in India for non-tradable goods are a fraction of US prices. Thus real incomes are higher in dollar terms than what would be indicated by the exchange rate. In view of this, the World Bank and IMF have been conducting a series of studies of incomes of countries based on the concept of purchasing power parity (PPP). This takes into account how much a certain amount of money can actually buy in India and what the cost of that bundle of goods would be in the USA. This increases Indian incomes several-fold compared to that indicated by the exchange rate. The per capita income for India at present is around $300 on an exchange rate basis but it rises to $1230 on a PPP basis, over four times. This suggests that $1 = Rs 8.40 is a more meaningful rate when converting rupees into dollars.
5. Official estimates of female-headed families in India are around 10 percent, but the actual incidence is considerably higher, possibly as much as 30 percent, especially in the rural areas (see BRIDGE. 1995. 'Background Paper on Gender Issues in India: Key Findings and Recommendations.' IDS, Sussex, p.7). Throughout the world, at least one third of households are headed by women who have sole responsibility for household production and needs (see Canadian Council for International Cooperation. 1991. ' "Two

Halves Make a Whole": Balancing Gender Relations in Development.' Ottawa, p.3).

6. Land is traditionally registered in the name of the eldest male household member and divided among his sons after his death. The law (varying according to the religion of the persons concerned) does allow for women to claim their share of property and land after the death of their fathers and husbands. In practice, however, this is rare. Women are either unaware of their legal rights or allow land and property to remain in men's hands in order to maintain goodwill and not alienate these relatives.

CHAPTER 2

The Business of Trafficking

WOMEN AND GIRLS continue to be misled and introduced into the sex trade by agents, in exchange for money. Trafficking is the systematic buying and selling of women and girls, and it continues despite being illegal under the Immoral Traffic in Persons (Prevention) Act (PITA) and the Indian Penal Code (IPC). Trafficking also operates internationally within an expanding network of supply, demand and transit of women and girls for commercial sex.

It should not be surprising that information about trafficking is hard to come by. When working with sex-workers we find that it is rare for them to open up and discuss frankly their personal experiences or their knowledge of how buying and selling operates. Sanlaap's information was gained during the course of implementing projects and doing crisis-intervention in the red-light areas. We have concentrated on verifying this information with the Sanlaap field staff and some key local people, and have also researched secondary sources. We feel that the police have more information but it is not openly available. Here we can present some figures and some evidence and highlight certain issues that need to be taken up for action. But we are able to throw only a little light on the subject by bringing these various sources together. It is not remarkable that so little is known about trafficking; more knowledge and far more action are required to stamp it out.

SURVEY RESULTS

Statistics of the number of women entering the profession through trafficking cannot be totally accurate because of the need for sex-workers to cover up their past, their reluctance to talk, and their concern to give a certain impression to the researcher. It is important to read the figures with this in mind, and to look beyond the simplification of giving just one reason as the main factor for joining the sex industry. The Sanlaap survey earlier cited in Chapter 1 found that 4.4 percent of women interviewed 'were sold into the profession'. It is possible that those who mentioned being brought by a friend or relative (4.4%), being cheated or misled (6.4%) and those who came with a husband or lover (5.4%) were all brought in through agents. Altogether this gives a total of 20.6 percent of respondents who mentioned a third person who might have been an agent and who could have taken money for introducing the woman to sex-work.

We have included relatives in this category of 'agent' because we have found that often a relative has contacts in the red-light areas. We have come across several cases where relatives have acted as agents and accepted payment for introducing the new workers. Husbands and lovers also hand over their partners in exchange for money, the 'husbands' sometimes being agents who go through a traditional marriage ceremony only to take a woman away from her community and bring her ultimately to a red-light area. Women who mentioned other social and economic factors, as stated in the survey, could also have been brought in by agents. In this way agents are seen as people who actively encourage and assist women to work in the sex trade, whether or not they gain from it financially. Table 2.1 is based on a 1988 survey by the All Bengal Women's Union. Of the 160 Calcutta sex-workers interviewed, 23 said they had come of their own accord, with friends or with some knowledge of the red-light area. The remaining 137 women were found to have been introduced into the sex trade by agents.

TABLE 2.1 Agents Introducing Women into the Sex Trade

1.	Neighbour in connivance with parents	7
2.	Neighbours as pimps (guardians not knowing)	19
3.	Aged sex-workers from same village or locality	31
4.	Unknown person/accidental meeting with pimp	32
5.	Mother/sister/near relative in the profession	18
6.	Lover giving false hope of marriage or job and selling to brothel	14
7.	Close acquaintance/near relative giving false hope of marriage or job	11
8.	'Husband' (not legally married)	3
9.	Husband (legally married)	1
10.	Young college student selling to brothel and visiting free of cost	1
	Total number through agents	137

Source: All-Bengal Women's Union, 1988.

This study also did a sex-wise disaggregation of the data: 76 percent of the agents were female, 24 percent male. Females may predominate because they can more easily befriend women and take them away without suspicion, especially when coming from countries such as Bangladesh where male-female relations are very restricted, and many male agents go through a pretence marriage ceremony or relationship in order to take the women away from their families. The figures also show that many of these agents are elderly sex-workers (19.4%). Elderly women can easily take on the role of a friend or a guardian of young women without arousing suspicion. The survey results also show that over 80 percent of the agents bringing women into the sex trade were known people: neighbours, relatives or other acquaintances.

TRAFFICKING IN ACTION

Working in the Calcutta red-light areas we have identified three types of procurers, all acting closely together to traffic women and children. The first are those based in the villages or towns, close to the homes of the women and children. These procurers are usually women who look out for economically and socially vulnerable girls, talking to them and their families and suggesting marriage or work in Calcutta. They then put them in touch with the middlemen who receive these girls. It is usually these middlemen who take the girls to the city, although sometimes the village-based procurers themselves deliver the girls directly to the cities. We know of many cases where young girls were married off in haste to unknown men as soon as they reached puberty. The 'grooms' may or may not have had sex with their new 'wives' before selling them off to the buyers in the red-light areas. Sometimes dowry is given to these 'grooms' by the parents of the girls, which is kept by the middlemen, along with money they are given when they hand them over to those directly involved in the sex trade. Many of the middlemen are sons of sex-workers or men brought up in the red-light areas, who also do other work such as bringing clients, protecting certain mashis and working in local political youth clubs. The final link is the person based in the red-light area itself, who 'purchases' the woman from the middleman. These are the people we encounter in our work. In Calcutta this is frequently a woman, known as the mashi, who is in need of a new girl. The mashi, often a former sex-worker in need of income, or even a middle-aged practising sex-worker, will pay for a new woman or a minor girl who will start to work as her maid. Later, when past puberty, this girl will be initiated into the trade. Men also receive new women, especially in Sonagachhi and Kidderpore where they maintain the women, bring in their clients, and take all or part of their income in exchange.

The middlemen are the essential link between the red-light areas and the villages. With help from local contacts they identify the girls who may be supplied to the sex trade and match this with the demand coming from the mashis and pimps. These middlemen are professionals in the art of deception. They build up contacts in places where they know there is poverty and deprivation, where parents cannot afford to be cautious and girls are easily tempted or are desperate for work. They offer friendship, marriage, jobs, or the opportunity to become a film star in the big city. They head for places where jobs are hard to get, and people are willing to migrate elsewhere; places hit by natural or political disasters which create refugees, homelessness and destroy people's livelihoods. They know the places where parents are not sufficiently protective, at least not of the girl child, where she is seen as a burden to be offloaded onto someone else. Former sex-workers, now aged, and mashis will visit their own and neighbouring villages to find new young women: sex-workers under a particular mashi are frequently from the same area. The majority of sex-workers who come to Calcutta via trafficking are not kidnapped but are lured, coaxed and cajoled with false promises or some offer of help out of a dead end or a crisis situation. Force, if used at all, is used later after the women have already been sold. Mashis themselves use friendship, sympathy, also veiled threats to convince the women that it is now in their interest to conform and begin working. It becomes risky for the women to leave, and they know that opportunities outside are also limited. Moreover, staying in the profession means acceptance within a community. Those few girls who do not conform are eventually threatened with violence, denied food, and, as a last resort, most mashis have access to gangs of hooligans who are used to intimidate the women or even inflict violence. Young girls, particularly ones who have been given away by their parents or have no families to return to, come around easily because of the sheer lack of alternatives. They are quite helpless and know only too well that mainstream society is unlikely to accept them back once they have lived in a red-light area.

The buying and selling aspect of trafficking is a system of payment for the procurer's work of finding, cajoling, perhaps marrying, and then transporting the woman. We feel it is seen by the procurer as her/his income for this work rather than as a price for the woman. But in fact the woman does become a commodity, and the amounts that change hands depend on the woman's capacity to earn money for others. The prices depend upon the women's age, complexion, looks, physique and where she is sold to. According to a study by Rozario (1988), the highest amounts change hands in Delhi and Bombay. The amount paid in exchange for the woman usually becomes her debt to be paid off to the mashi or the pimp.

The informal network of trafficking provides an occasional income to people associated with the sex trade. Most mashis are themselves former sex-workers who have no other means of income, and who return to their villages to bring new girls into the sex trade. A few years ago parents of two girls from Murshidabad came to the Bowbazar red-light area in search of their daughters who had gone missing just the day before. They were quickly put in touch with the local club boys and some activists (local residents and leaders who also work for NGOs), who helped them to find out who had recently returned from a trip to Murshidabad. They were finally put in touch with an elderly mashi. The local activists, along with the parents, went to the mashi's house and found that the two girls were indeed there. They were quickly and quietly handed over. All this took just a couple of hours.

A worker from an outside NGO suggested that the police be brought in, but the parents were not interested and quickly returned to Murshidabad with the girls, hoping to hush it all up. Although the mashi was legally committing an offence, nobody felt that it would be appropriate to involve the police or take any action against her. Within the red-light areas the work of the mashis is generally not viewed as unacceptable, unless they have used particularly harsh methods to force new girls into the trade against their will. Most parents would prefer to hush up incidents where their own daughters became linked with the sex trade in some way or the other, rather than take action against the perpetrators.

International trafficking seems to be on the rise. Women and children are traded from one country to another, and customers even come from abroad to use them. Other Asian countries such as Thailand and the Philippines now find themselves facing both an outflow of their female citizens and an influx of foreign nationals in the business of sexual exploitation. Minor girls and women from remote tribal areas are tricked into joining the trade to cater to the increasing demand from customers. Asian women abroad are confined against their will and have their passports confiscated. Forms of trafficking range from mail-order bride syndicates, forced marriages, abuse of entertainment workers, to contract work as domestic helpers, all of which can result in sexual exploitation and yet occur under the legal cover of 'labour migration' (Sancho 1994).

To understand the international scenario clearly, countries have been categorized as sending, transit or receiving centres for the trafficking of women and children. India is mainly a receiving country, a reception centre for women from Bangladesh and Nepal. It also acts as a transit country and, being so large, has its own internal sending, transit and receiving areas. Calcutta itself is an important receiver. It also functions as a transit place from where Indian, Bangladeshi and Nepalese women who come to the city, either independently or through agents, are taken to red-light areas in other cities such as Bombay, or even to other countries in the Middle East.

Receiving Centre

The story of Maya is not atypical:

> I came from Bangladesh many years ago. A group of us were brought by some men, and I was the youngest. I can't even remember my family or my village now. When we arrived in Calcutta we were split up and I was sent to work as a maid. The house was in a red-light area and here I spent my childhood. When my periods started coming I was brought to this place and lived with another woman who brought me into this trade. I worked here for a while and was also taken to Bombay. Although I made more money in Bombay I prefer this place, I know every lane and I know all the people. I am popular with some regular clients, even though I am getting on a bit. I don't remember how many years I have been working on the line.[1]

Bunu was brought to India from Nepal through trafficking. She was eleven when she left her village in Nepal in search of work. She was befriended by a young man who promised to help her find work and brought her to Kamathipura, a well-known red-light area in Bombay. He took her to meet some of his friends, and there she was sold to a woman who ran a brothel. She was not allowed to leave the house. Kept under strict vigilance with constant intimidation and threats, she was initiated into the sex industry. After three long years— long enough to more than pay back her debt to the madam— she was allowed to return home. She gave an honest account

of her story to her relatives, but they had no sympathy for
her and she was given a cold reception. Realizing that she
was no longer welcome at home, she returned to India. Someone had told her that people in the Calcutta red-light areas
were kinder than those in Bombay, and so she came here. She
was still only fourteen, but had discovered that a red-light
area would be her only home. She still works in the same
red-light area in the mornings, practising elsewhere in the
afternoons, sharing a room and working in the aadhiya system. She earns Rs.50 to 100 a day.

It is estimated that roughly 100,000 to 160,000 Nepalese
girls and women are working as sex-workers in India. Roughly
20 percent of them are estimated to be under twenty years of
age, with 35 percent abducted under the pretext of marriage
or jobs (study by Thapa 1989; quoted in Jyoti and Poudel
1994: 2). Five thousand to 7,000 young Nepalese girls are said
to be trafficked every year to various red-light areas in India
(ABC, Nepal 1993; quoted in Jyoti and Poudel 1994 : 2). Many
of these Nepalese women who are being brought to Calcutta
will have first come to Sonagachhi or Kidderpore, and will
later move to other red-light areas. Studies on trafficking from
Nepal to India have specifically mentioned the open border
between the two countries as a major factor facilitating trafficking of women (Jyoti and Poudel 1994 : 8).

While other Asian countries have discovered organized rack-
ets where false papers are procured for women, or where women
are given travel documents to work as 'entertainers' in receiving
countries (such as Germany, Holland and Japan), India receives
women without such formality. Nepalese and Indians do not
need visas to cross the border between the two countries. The
Bangladesh border is not open but quite easy to cross even without the correct papers. Activists working in Bangladesh on the
issue have reported that the border areas of Satkhira, Jessore,
Meherpur, Kusthia, Chapai Nawabganj, Dinajpur, Kurigram
and Lalmonirhat are used as land crossings for women being
trafficked from Bangladesh to India (Ain O Salish Kendro 1994)
(see Map).

In a report to the Bangladesh High Commission in Calcutta
in 1989, Shib Sankar Chakroborty,[2] a lawyer working with
women survivors of trafficking, stated that the Bangladesh

Rifles (BDR) men take between Taka 200-500 per head (Bangladeshi currency) for crossing the border, while the Indian Border Security Force (BSF) charge Rs.100-250 (which then came to the same amount in value). He also reports that sexual assault of illegal female immigrants by the police at the border is commonplace. We have had such complaints from many sex-workers too. Some women had their first experience of 'trading' their bodies when they were raped by the police at the border for failing to pay the money they would need to buy their way into India (Chakroborty, *Amrita Bazar Patrika*, 9 April 1989).

Indrani Sinha made a visit to Bongaon near the Bangladesh-India border. The border was busy with waiting trucks, customs staff and money-changers. The BSF post was crowded with tired men and women crossing over to India. Local auto-rickshaw drivers, handling agents and small hotel-keepers reported that men accompanying girls and women across the border was a common sight, and that these men did not even bother with forged documents, they handed over the money quite openly as they came across the border. The Bangladesh border is simply a wire fence which is easy to cross at night. One man who has run auto-rickshaws from the Bongaon-Bangladesh border to the Bongaon train station for fifteen years said that it is easier to cross from the official entry points staffed by the border police than to cross the fence at night. He said the villagers will shout and stop you if they catch you crossing at night, but the police will simply take money and let you go. Local people related that the BSF had prior information of when the trafficking agents would be coming. The same agents come each time so they have become quite familiar in the locality, and the people seem to know about the purpose of their visit. The women sometimes change hands after crossing the border, where a new agent transports them to Bongaon station and then on to Calcutta.

Women arriving in this way, in small groups, are taken to places like the Eden Gardens, Maidan and parks around the Esplanade area,[3] where the deals are made which seal their futures. They may change hands around four or five times before being finally settled into their new working lives. We have heard that pimps from Kidderpore buy directly from the Esplanade parks and Eden Gardens which are regular selling points.

We established contact with Amar, a young man who was born and brought up in one of the main red-light areas in Calcutta, quite easily. He told us that his mother too originates from the same area. Amar has a relationship with a woman who makes a living renting out her one room to three sex-workers. He told us some things about trafficking as he has seen quite a lot happen in the area. He sees very young Nepalese girls being brought in by agents. He has even seen girls being brought in by their parents. He confirms that final settlements take place outside the red-light area, mentioning the infamous park. This place is so near the courts, the government offices and Lalbazar police headquarters, yet this proximity appears to make no difference.

Sending Out

Women are also sent from Calcutta to other places. In 1988 a case came to light where young girls were being sold from Presidency Jail in Calcutta to some Bombay brothels. Four Bangladeshi women, in jail because of illegal immigration, were released by an agent at Basirhat Court, in the North 24-Parganas district, who was paid Rs.5,000 for each woman by another agent who transported the women and sold them to brothels in Bombay. One of these women, Praveen Khatoon, escaped and returned to Calcutta where she exposed the network. Shib Sankar Chakroborty took up the case despite threats from influential traffickers. The same lawyer also exposed a racket where jail employees posed as mothers of young female inmates and applied for their custody, only to sell the girls into prostitution immediately after their release from the government-run homes. Men and women posing in court as relatives to take away girls to the red-light areas are part of a well-organized racket.

Recent cases have been reported in the press; for example, an organized racket smuggling girls from the north of West Bengal to Bombay (*The Telegraph*, 20 November 1995) and another racket of smugglers taking girls from Howrah district in West Bengal to Bombay. In the former case, a girl was rescued from a Bombay brothel by a client and reported that she had been taken with the false promise of a job as a domestic worker, and then sold for Rs.40,000. She had seen many girls from her home district in the Bombay brothels.

Cases have been reported of women and girls from West Bengal being sold to both national and international markets. Rozario (1988) reported a network where young Bengali girls were taken by agents to Kashmir for work but were actually sold off as 'brides' to the Gulf. A nine year old was sold to a forty-year-old man, a fifteen year old to a sixty-year-old man. One girl was discovered in a hotel after having been locked up for nine months while her documents and passage were being arranged. Cases of poor Muslim minors being taken abroad through marriage deals are heard of quite regularly.

FORMAL NETWORKS

The north Indian state of Uttar Pradesh (UP) is allegedly the centre of organized selling, especially Allahabad, Varanasi, Lucknow and Kanpur (Rozario 1988). We ourselves are aware of a well-organized network where children and young women are brought to Calcutta from UP. Young Bengali girls are known to have been bought under this system, taken to UP where they are raised to be returned and sold to brothels in Calcutta later. Some communities within red-light areas have their own trafficking networks which run their own panchayat[4] and are highly organized, preventing entrance to any outsiders. One particular panchayat is so organized that it has its own pimps. It owns property and controls landlords in the area and is managing to expel sex-workers from different communities, replacing them with its own women in order gradually to expand its influence in the area.

Organized networks which operate nationally are known to sell and re-sell women, moving them around different areas and booking large profits each time. Jyotsna Chatterjee of the Joint Women's Programme in Delhi has worked with sex-workers for years, and reports:

> Sometimes mini-bus loads of girls are brought by pimps from [such] markets. One of our field workers had wit-

nessed the arrival of a mini-bus full of girls from south Nepal who were brought to a house in the red-light area near the city centre in Allahabad (Chatterjee 1984: 3).

In our work we have rarely come across the organized trafficking networks. The existence of formal networks is widely acknowledged by the sex-workers, however. Access to this world is difficult as the girls are heavily guarded and even afterwards, when working independently, they are reluctant to discuss their experiences. Police do uncover networks from time to time and these are reported in the media.

STATE INVOLVEMENT

Undoubtedly the most shocking and depressing aspect of the sex trade is the involvement of individuals who represent the state as police, politicians and the border police, and other powerful vested interest groups, including influential people. An excellent study on the implementation of prostitution and trafficking laws between 1980-1987, conducted by Jean D'Cunha throws light on the state's inability or reluctance to clamp down on trafficking. D'Cunha found that only 535 of the alleged 50,000 brothels in Bombay were raided during the seven-year period of her study. While many sex-workers were arrested, no pimps or landlords were, and of those brothel-keepers and procurers arrested, all were released on bail after which the majority of the cases were either dropped or the offenders were untraceable. She cites the main reasons for the tardy implementation as 'the economic and political linkages between the prostitution racketeers, the police, and local bigwigs' (1988: 228). On top of the regular bribe received by police officers in some areas, the discovery of new minors brought into the trade is a lucrative business. In the well-known case of a Nepalese child, Tulasa, who was discovered by the Bombay police, the latter demanded Rs.700 to turn a blind eye. Their silence was bargained down to Rs.500 by the brothel-owner.[5] D'Cunha estimated that the monthly income of the Vigilance Crime Branch, Bombay, in 1988 from such sources was Rs.100,000.

We have ourselves experienced cases where the police manipulate information to protect traffickers. In one case, a group of four men and women brought a new Nepalese girl to a Calcutta red-light area and asked a local woman if she wanted her for a price. This person was also a local social activist, and so feigning interest, she began to negotiate, having sent for assistance in the meantime. Other activists came, confronted the agents and managed to capture one of them. They took the girl and the man to the police station. Activists sat with the girl throughout her interview with the police. She repeatedly said she was fifteen, but the police recorded her age as 'around eighteen'. This was pointed out at the time and the police agreed to correct it. However, they ultimately submitted the report with the incorrect age. As a result the girl was sent to the government Liluah Home for adults, from where she would have been sent to court and quickly released back to the agents. We later discovered that the agent who tried to sell her had been released on bail with only a petty charge against him. We know of several such cases where procurers and anti-socials are charged with petty, reduced cases by the police and then released with a small fine.

The police deliberately and knowingly recorded misinformation about the girl's age, despite her insistence that she was younger, and it was clear that she was younger than eighteen. Perhaps police register minors as adults because it is easier to release adults, who then fall straight back into the hands of the pimps and traffickers. Juveniles are dealt with by juvenile courts and welfare boards which are more specialized, and are supposed to investigate the girl's family circumstances and background. We have been told by a senior policeman who deals in many cases related to the sex trade that minors rescued from the sex trade cannot go through the Juvenile Courts because they are not classed as juvenile delinquents. The Juvenile Justice Act (1986), however, specifically covers 'neglected children' who are 'likely to be exploited for immoral purposes' or are living in brothels; and these children are supposed to be produced before Juvenile Welfare Boards, five of which exist in West Bengal. Significantly, the charges are more severe for the offence of trafficking of minors: up to fourteen years imprisonment for trafficking of seventeen or eighteen year olds, and up to life imprisonment for trafficking of anyone aged sixteen or under, whether or not they consented. The traffickers clearly benefit if minors are recorded as aged over eighteen. Are the agents known to the police, and are they actively doing deals with them? We have to entertain this possibility because the police certainly have no other explanation. In the case just discussed, the agent was charged with a minor and unrelated offence and easily released; this points to police collaboration with the traffickers.

It is common knowledge among NGOs and the staff of welfare homes that false 'parents'—different people on different occasions—come to claim young sex-workers on their release from the court. Either extreme indifference or cooperation with these so-called parents must explain the court's failure to identify the 'parents' as agents, mashis or traffickers. Acknowledging the problems, the law actually calls for a special investigation by a social welfare organization to establish the identities of guardians claiming back minors from red-light areas (Section 17A of PITA). This is rarely if ever implemented, and the release simply depends on a report by a probation officer. We are certain that the report can be influenced for a price. There have been cases where even sex-workers publicly 'rescued' by lawyers or NGOs have simply been claimed back by agents of the sex industry posing as guardians.

We met twenty-three Nepalese girls at the Liluah Home, the government remand home for adult women. It was a strange case. The girls had all been rounded up during a raid in Sonagachhi and their reports said they had been caught as minor prostitutes. A couple could have been around seventeen years old, but some were even as young as twelve or thirteen. One girl could not even wear the dirty white saree she had been issued at the Home, she just held it bunched up at the waist. But one of the older girls, an old hand at this routine, assured us: 'Our people will come, the bail papers will be ready, and they will say they are our mothers or our aunts. We will agree. I have been through this before. We will all be out of here within three weeks.' And she was right. Gradually their cases went to court, a few at a time, and they were released.

We took the opportunity to ask them about their backgrounds. The younger ones would not even speak. The others told us that they had all come from Nepal at one time or another, being picked up from villages one by one, and then had travelled in small groups with a few other girls and some men. They were all working in Sonagachhi in different houses. When we asked their names they kept changing them, making fun or forgetting which name they had given to the Home. They had been brought in by women police officers, but had not been examined to determine their age or injuries arising from sexual abuse, although this is required under the law (Section 15 of PITA). By this time they were all saying they were over eighteen. The anomaly was that, although the charges against them related to their being minors, they had not been brought in front of the Juvenile Welfare Board, even though by law all 'neglected children' should be brought up before the Juvenile Welfare Board, and by law a recognized social welfare agency should investigate the identities of the 'guardians' of these girls.

Apart from the occasional raid, the authorities appear to be doing very little actively to stop trafficking. We have been told by several senior policemen that they raid only when they receive a complaint or information about a new minor coming into an area. Even then it is the girl who is the focus of the intervention and not the agents.

Our work as a NGO that would like to stop trafficking is severely restricted in Calcutta because the law and order situation is heavily influenced by politics and corruption. We cannot count on the support of the police and politicians. This is despite senior-level commitment to our work. The situation is a complex one and, to give an example, if we were to take support from the police to rescue a bonded woman from a red-light area, the effort could be counter-productive in the long run. We could be thrown out of the area, unable to continue our work. The police would not be able to help us then. Criminality is a great concern in these areas. Mafia-type networks are becoming more widespread and effective. These networks encompass the local forces, mainly police and hoodlums, and are linked with drugs and alcohol dealing as well as the trafficking of women. It is ironic that those who should be bringing the culprits to book are often powerless, and some even have a stake in the crime. Linkages between politicians and anti-socials are to their mutual benefit. Politicians who court the most influential anti-socials, including traffickers, guarantee themselves a vote bank, and links between the two reinforce the power of each.

The evidence thus points to a heavy reliance on agents in the sex industry to bring in a high turnover of new women and girls. While the majority of these agents seem to operate independently and informally, organized networks do also exist, and are aided by the collaboration of individuals working in the state institutions. At the very least they may accept money to turn a blind eye and let off trafficking agents on petty charges. Thus a pointless cycle of raids to channel sexworkers through rescue homes and courts continues, skirting around the edges of the trafficking network but failing to make any dent whatsoever. Votebanks are to be maintained and the interests of powerful groups protected, and all this goes on at the expense of the women and girls who are treated as commodities to be bought and sold. Large sums of money change hands on a regular basis, the greater the violation of human rights the more clandestine the operation and the larger the amounts involved. Trafficking is no doubt a lucrative business for those who engage in this trade. Indeed, UN rapporteur Jean Ferant has gone on record saying that traffic in women is more profitable than arms or drug smuggling (Sancho 1994).

India has made commitments to eliminate trafficking. India was a signatory to the United Nations International Convention for the Suppression of Traffic in Persons and of the Exploitation of Others (1950) and as a result the SITA legislation (1956, now known as PITA) was passed. SITA penalizes procuring and detaining women and girls for sex-work. India has also ratified the treaty of the Convention on the Elimination of All Forms of Discrimination Against Women (1979) during the UN Decade for Women. This obligates the government to suppress all forms of traffic in women. In 1990 India signed the Geneva Human Rights treaty which also prohibited trafficking in women and children as a human rights violation.

The worth of these conferences and treaties has to be questioned in the light of the government's apparent failure to tackle trafficking. How can we take these declarations of commitment forward? From the grass roots to the policy level these documents can be used as tools for awareness—raising and lobbying about the government's stated ideals. Internal as well as international pressure can be brought on the government and police to implement it's anti-trafficking stand. A combined approach is needed to educate sex-workers about their legal rights and the laws on trafficking, and to coordinate with local police stations or thanas to try and create more respect, trust and dialogue between sex-workers and the local police. Senior police officials, lawyers and the media need to be involved in this process. Alternative livelihoods need to be explored for former sex-workers who are themselves turning to trafficking. Women's groups in the red-light areas can monitor the arrival of new girls and develop a system of preventing forced entry into the profession at the point of reception. (This has already happened in the Kalighat red-light area, see Chapter 8.) It is hoped that some clarity and some action will emerge to eliminate these abuses of human rights and abuses of the law which have been tolerated for so long. It is simply not enough to focus merely on rescuing a few individuals.

NOTES

1. When the sex-workers are soliciting clients they stand lining the sides of the lanes of the red-light areas. This is referred to as 'the line', and women refer to 'working on the line' or becoming a 'line-woman'.

2. Shib Sankar Chakroborty, an independent lawyer, has been involved in several legal cases concerning the rescue of sex-workers from bonded labour in some Calcutta red-light areas with the help of local residents.

3. Calcutta's city centre is dominated by a large open green space called the Maidan, which is used for cricket, grazing animals, street trade by hawkers as well as other more grim purposes like selling of young girls to pimps, drug peddling and so on. The Eden Gardens is Calcutta's famous cricket ground which, along with the Esplanade area, borders the Maidan to the north.

4. An elected community-level decision-making body. The term is used in this context to denote that a similar form of local government exists in some red-light areas.
5. Tulasa was a minor girl rescued from bonded labour in a brothel in Bombay. Her rescue, emotional return home to Nepal and her rehabilitation there were extensively publicized in the Indian press.

CHAPTER 3

The Double Standards of the Law

> 'The prostitute is not at all a criminal. She does not violate anybody or anything, but is herself violated.'
>
> — Jean D'Cunha

THE PRESENT LAW ensures that the sex trade is accessible but not offensively public and that sex-workers are allowed to work but without legal protection. No other profession suffers from such a confusion about what is legal and what is illegal, nor is any other worker punished only when her/his profession is visible to the public. The impact of these laws on the sex-workers themselves is considered of secondary importance to maintaining society's sexual double standards.

Legal approaches to prostitution can be broadly divided into three categories: legalization, prohibition and toleration. Legalization accepts the institution of prostitution and gives full legal rights to sex-workers, often accompanied by registration, licensing and compulsory medical check-ups. This is practised in West Germany and the state of Nevada in the USA. Prohibition totally criminalizes the activities of all categories of people related to the sex trade such as pimps, brothel-keepers and clients. This approach exists in all other states of America and in Japan. The third approach is that of tolerance, which criminalizes the organizers of the sex trade but not the sex-

Which one?

workers themselves. This is intended to suppress prostitution gradually by tackling the exploitative elements without harming the sex-workers. An important United Nations Convention in 1949 promoted the toleration approach, which was later adopted by many countries such as the UK and India. India's legal approach is one of limited tolerance, where being a sex-worker per se is not an offence, and practising sex-work privately and independently is also not a crime. But practising and soliciting in or near a public place is a punishable offence; the sex-worker's punishment is less harsh than that of her landlord, the manager of a brothel, or someone accused of trafficking. The legal rights of sex-workers include the rights to rescue and rehabilitation. Sex-workers do have the right to police protection just like any other citizen. They can also, with support, take advantage of existing loopholes and contradictions in the law to achieve some basic rights.

but not implemented

rights are not legally

INDIA'S LEGAL SYSTEM

The current legislation in India in the form of the Immoral Traffic in Persons (Prevention) Act (PITA) provides for punishment of sex-workers who do not keep their profession hidden from 'the public,' and deals with the excesses of exploitation in the industry. Sex-work is tolerated, meaning that it is neither legal nor illegal: sex-workers are not committing a crime when they practise privately and independently, but they cannot solicit legally in public. In theory sex-workers are left alone to carry on with their work provided it is not within 200 metres of a public place. Like other informal sector self-employed workers, they are not entitled to child-care facilities, compensation or minimum wages.

India's legal approach towards prostitution has shifted since the nineteenth century from legalization to toleration. Socially, zones of tolerance known as red-light areas have always existed, but the legal status of the sex-workers has altered. The swings in the legal approach to sex-work reflect both the practical and moral preoccupations of the state. The dual perception of sex-workers as fulfilling a useful role in society on the one hand and being a corruptive influence on the other results in a dilemma that is reflected in the confused legal approach to sex-work. The law has to cater to a public demand for both condemnation and toleration. What has been consistent is that then, as now, regulations and prohibitions have been concerned to a greater extent with maintaining a hypocritical public morality than with the protection or welfare of the sex-workers themselves. Just seventy years ago Calcutta had a special Moral Police Force to supervise and control brothels and prostitutes.

During the British period the first legislation on prostitution was passed. The Contagious Diseases Acts, 1869, were British acts that applied to all countries falling under British rule. Sex-workers were required to register with the police, and they had to submit to regular medical examinations. Those suffering from sexually transmitted diseases were confined to special 'lock' hospitals until they were cured. They were taken there forcibly if they refused to go, resulting in many women going underground or evading registration. In 1879 the Calcutta Commissioner of Police complained that while the number of registered sex-workers was decreasing, the number of registered brothels increased from 2,420 at the beginning of the year to 2,458 at the end (Chatterjee 1992 : 12). This interest in the health of the sex-workers grew out of the concern for the health of the British soldiers who were regular visitors to the brothels. The sex-workers were thus viewed in early legislation primarily as disease-carriers. This controversial act was suspended in 1883 following campaigns by elite women who found the involvement of the state in such 'immoral' activities abhorrent, and who advocated the suppression of prostitution. Various state bills and acts were then passed that attempted to abolish brothels, trafficking and soliciting, although success in this field was always elusive. The Indian Penal Code (IPC) continued to criminalize trafficking, and clauses regarding public indecency and public nuisance could be used against the sex-workers themselves.

Later, as a direct result of India being a signatory to a United Nations declaration in 1950 in New York on the suppression of trafficking, the All-India Suppression of Immoral Traffic Act 1956 (SITA) was passed. This was later amended in 1986 to the now current PITA. Both intended to abolish organized prostitution gradually by criminalizing pimps, landlords, brothel-keepers and traffickers. Ironically, PITA allows for toleration of red-light areas by hitting at sex-workers who are visible in a 'public place', in effect confining them to areas where 'the public' are not offended and will not complain. As mentioned earlier, sex-workers can be prosecuted only if they solicit or practise in or within 200 metres of a public place or notified area. (A notified area is a place that is declared as prostitution-free by the state government under the PITA. None exists in West Bengal.) However, even if a woman does not solicit or practise in a public place, the law continues to stigmatize her, for example, by criminalizing living with or being in the habitual company of a sex-worker (Section 4.2 (a) of PITA) and by giving power to the state to remove a child who lives with a sex-worker or in a brothel from the red-light area. One who visits places used by sex-workers or associates with any person who leads an immoral, drunken or depraved life is also criminalized (Section 15(2) of the Juvenile Justice Act). Moreover, sex-workers can be removed from any place at the request of a magistrate (Section 20, PITA). The spirit and objectives of SITA were maintained in the 1986 PITA amendment and various technical changes were introduced. For example, the definition of prostitution was changed from when a girl or woman 'offers her body for promiscuous intercourse for hire' to 'the sexual exploitation or abuse of persons for commercial purposes'. PITA also takes a more serious view of the prostitution of minors, and introduces the requirement that two female police officers must be present on brothel-raids. Only women police officers are now supposed to interrogate women and girls who have been removed from brothels.

The legal status of prostitution in India not only has a significant impact on the lives of those involved in the sex trade, but also reflects the current attitudes of the state and of mainstream society towards prostitution. The extent of women's involvement in illegal activities is significantly affected by whether or not prostitution is considered an offence. In India, among female offenders, the majority are involved in the sex trade. In 1989 arrests under PITA were only 0.4 percent of all crimes, yet the highest number of women arrested in this category of local and special laws was under this act. In the same year, the highest number of women arrested under the Indian

Penal Code was for the trafficking of women and girls ('Crime in India', Ministry of Home Affairs, National Crime Records Bureau, New Delhi, 1989).

The main points of the current PITA legislation are as follows:

Sex-workers. Carrying on prostitution in or within 200 metres of a public place or within a notified area, and soliciting or seduction in public, or in sight or sound of a public place for the purpose of prostitution are offences under Sections 7 and 8. Public place is defined as any place intended for use by, or accessible to, the public and includes any public conveyance. Working privately and independently as a prostitute is not an offence. However, a sex-worker can be removed from any place at the request of a magistrate, and a brothel containing two or more sex-workers can be closed down.

Clients. The client commits an offence if he carries on prostitution with a sex-worker in or within 200 metres of a public place, or in a notified area. (Under the Indian Penal Code, if the sex-worker is below sixteen the client can be charged with rape.)

Babus. Live-in babus or lovers are committing an offence by living off the earnings of prostitution. If any babu who is proved to be living with a sex-worker is arrested under these charges, he is assumed to be living off her earnings unless he can prove otherwise.

Brothel-keepers. A brothel is defined as any place 'used for sexual exploitation or abuse, for the gain of another person or for the mutual gain of two or more prostitutes'. Landlords, brothel-keepers and those who abet brothel-keeping can be punished under Section 3 of the act. Detaining a person for prostitution is also an offence. A magistrate can order the closure of a brothel that is within 200 metres of a public place. Hotels that are being used as brothels can have their licenses suspended or cancelled if any of the sex-workers are minors.

Landlords. Knowingly renting out property which is being used for prostitution is an offence under Section 7.

Traffickers. Procuring, inducing, taking or detaining a person for prostitution are offences under Section 5. If the person is a minor or a child, or if the person was procured against her will, the sentence is more severe.

Pimps. Pimping and touting is an offence under Section 4. It is assumed, unless proved otherwise, that a pimp is living wholly or partially on the earnings of a sex-worker.

Rescued Girls. The government is bound to provide rehabilitation in a protective institution, or under the supervision of a person appointed by the magistrate, for women and girls rescued from prostitution.

Under the Juvenile Justice Act children of sex-workers and minors, classified as vulnerable because they associate with sex-workers, can be removed to a registered Juvenile Home (government or NGO) until they come of age.

The IPC includes separate offences that cover sex-workers, traffickers and clients who have sex with minor girls. Either the IPC or the PITA can be used, although the IPC is more commonly used because it is easier to prove. PITA crimes tend to be more specific and require stricter formalities on behalf of the police.

The IPC sections which are commonly used are:

Committing public nuisance (Section 290) or performing an obscene act in a public place (Section 294);

Procuring and kidnapping women and girls (Sections 361, 363, 366, 366a and 366b);

Rape of a minor, or sex with a woman who believes the man is her husband (Section 375);

Importing a woman under twenty-one from another country for sexual purposes (Section 366h).

It is ironic that sex-workers are prevented from soliciting in public places, when those public places often have a direct link with the sex trade. For example, we have already described how the Kalighat red-light area grew up around the Kalighat Temple to cater to the pilgrims and travellers who came to stay in the *dharamshalas* . The history of the two has been linked since the temple was built, and the legislation criminalizing soliciting near a temple come along much later—the temple and its vicinity became a 'public place'.

IMPLEMENTATION OF THE LAW

A feature of the toleration system worldwide has been that in its implementation it has been used mostly against the sex-workers themselves. By far the majority of arrests in India, under SITA, have been of women charged under Sections 7 and 8. Jean D'Cunha conducted an intensive study in Bombay into the implementation of the laws on prostitution between the years 1980-1987, and found that 596 brothel-keepers were arrested during the period compared to 9,240 sex-workers. Only 304 procurers were arrested in the period 1980-1984, while not one pimp or landlord was arrested during those four years. Looking at the number of arrests under the Bombay Police Act sections dealing with 'indecent' behaviour, she found that 1,395 pimps were held, as compared to 53,866 sex-workers between 1980 and 1987 (D'Cunha 1991:50).

In West Bengal, for which we have more recent data, we find that far more women are arrested than men under PITA. During 1989, in West Bengal 80 percent of arrests under PITA were of women (Ministry of Home Affairs, 1989). In 1992, 71 women and 12 men were arrested, in 1993 the number of women was 129, against 46 men, 66 women and 22 men in 1994, and in 1995, up to 31 July, 40 women and 20 men were arrested.[1] Aside from these figures, sex-workers are regularly taken in by the police and they have to hand over some money in return for their release, a practice which is never, of course, revealed in statistics.

Although the intention of the Prevention of Immoral Traffic Act was to decriminalize the sex-workers and hit hardest at the traffickers, pimps and brothel-keepers, in practice the opposite has happened. The two clauses affecting the women have been widely used while the rest have been almost ineffective. While disaggregated figures for crimes within PITA are not available for West Bengal, our experience would suggest that the majority of the women arrested under PITA in West Bengal were sex-workers rather than mashis or landladies. D'Cunha cites several reasons why a higher number of sex-workers are arrested: mass arrests help to maintain arrest quotas—many members of the police force have openly said that they have to show a certain number of cases in their record regularly and so they arrest sex-workers, who are easy targets; the police stand to gain financially: the arrests are often a form of harassment accompanying extortion and sex-favours; brothel-keepers instigate arrest of those sex-workers whom they want to harass; the organizers of the sex trade get around the law by exploiting loopholes, bribing, and using muscle-power, whereas the sex-workers themselves are not organized enough to do so.

D'Cunha examines why the general implementation of the PITA is shoddy and ineffective: racketeering offences are bailable and the offenders cannot be traced subsequently; sex-workers' statements are inaccurately recorded so prosecutions are ineffective; clients are reluctant to act as witnesses and thus unreliable people are used to act as bogus clients and later these people also may not be available. Racketeers produce false age certificates so they cannot be charged with trafficking minors; women are intimidated into saying they are of age and are working independently; bribes are paid to drop cases. The sexist attitudes of magistrates influence their interpretation of the laws (D'Cunha 1991: 61).

SEX-WORKER'S RIGHTS

The intended spirit of toleration laws is to punish the organizers of the sex trade while allowing sex-workers themselves full rights as citizens. Because the actual PITA only espouses limited tolerance, the issue of sex-worker's rights is confusing and open to interpretation. For example, sex-workers living in brothels can be evicted by a magistrate with only seven days' notice, and any tenancy agreement they may possess can become null and void. Tenancy agreements under most state tenancy laws prohibit 'immoral' activities and commercial activities going on in residential areas, and PITA allows for sex-workers to be removed from any place at the request of a magistrate. Thus sex-workers practising privately and independently (and therefore legally) can still be evicted on the basis of their profession, although they will not be charged with having committed any crime. Secure tenancy and freedom from eviction are constitutional rights that are not granted to the sex-workers. We do know, however, of sex-workers who have fought successfully for water supply on the basis of legally valid rent agreements, and have maintained low rents under the West Bengal tenancy laws. Also, sex-workers have been granted ration cards and new voters' identity cards, both of which can be used to establish occupancy. The present Chief Election Commissioner, T. N. Seshan, stated that sex-workers were eligible for voters' identity cards. In Kalighat recently, two sex-workers were prevented from having their photographs taken for their voters' identity cards by some junior police officials. Several women protested, senior police officers had to intervene; the sex-workers received an apology and their photographs were taken. It is ironical that known sex-workers are allowed to vote in a particular ward on the basis of their residential addresses, although even to have a residential address is legally ambiguous.

An interesting case demonstrates how the law can also be used in the interest of the sex-workers. Recently, Bagherhat, a small red-light area of about fifty women on the outskirts of Calcutta, became the site of a struggle. Trouble began when a landlord split from a local political group and refused to give his payoff money to them while continuing to take money from his sex-worker tenants. Consequently, the political group, with support from an important political leader, threatened to evict the women and began intimidating them. Along with some local NGOs and activists from other red-light areas, the women demonstrated at the police station and demanded protection. On the day of the feared eviction, a lawyer filed a petition with a magistrate calling on the police to intervene to prevent a breach of peace. The lawyer argued in favour of the women that they had no place to go to and there was no rehabilitation available, and so their eviction by the local residents should be prevented. This was successfully argued and an agreement was reached between the two factions; the women were secure in their homes once again. The fact that they possessed ration cards was used as proof of their legitimate right to occupancy.[2] All this happened despite the fact that the same magistrate is actually empowered to close down brothels. In the light of such cases, we argue that sex-workers do have a right to use the law for their own protection.

Fighting for the constitutional rights of sex-workers as citizens can be a positive focus of legal struggles. For example, an organization of sex-workers and brothel-keepers in Delhi successfully fought for the right to admit their children to schools without having to give the name of the father on admission forms. Some Calcutta sex-workers recently formed the first registered society in the name of sex-workers. Existing rules stipulate that society members should be of good 'moral character', and because of this sex-workers have been prevented from forming societies in the past (except when they did not declare their profession). This time the sex-workers, along with staff from the AIIH&PH's STD and HIV Intervention Project, met with senior personnel in charge of registration and argued successfully that just because they were forced to earn a living in the sex trade, it did not mean that they were immoral people. This is ground-breaking work and reveals that sex-workers, with some amount of initial support from the outside, can successfully challenge their legal isolation.

ROLE OF THE POLICE

From our own experiences we have found that the police do support the existence of the sex trade and see their role mainly as eliminating excessive exploitation such as trafficking of minors. They are also concerned to keep the sex trade confined within the red-light areas and implement the laws usually when the women are too visible or when there are complaints from 'the public'. The extent of police cooperation with brothel-keepers and traffickers and their harassment of sex-workers is a reflection of the double standards of morality prevailing in the implementation of the law. Agents of the law are ordinary people, mostly men who have been brought up in this society that creates and tacitly accepts sex-work, while being unable to accept the sex-workers themselves. Just as the law itself is unable to resolve these contradictions, nor can the police officers, police chiefs or court functionaries. 'There are known cases of magistrates asking lawyers defending prostitutes in court to send the latter to them' (D'Cunha 1991: 64). There are also known cases of the police refusing to accept First Information Reports (FIRs) against traffickers. A woman who had escaped from a Bombay brothel returned to her home in West Bengal and informed against the local hoodlum who had sold her. Three villagers caught the man and took him to the police station. Refusing to accept a FIR, the police put the villagers in the lock-up instead! A subsequent enquiry found that 'a girl-running racket was thriving in Bagnan, Uluberia, Bavrai and Shankrail' (*The Telegraph*, 21 November 1995). Even senior police officers regard sex-workers rather than traffickers or the sex industry as a whole as the focus of legal intervention.

The law offers endless opportunities for the policemen to make money. Joarder spent many years studying the sex trade in Calcutta, and noted that it is common practice for the police to inform brothel-keepers how to avoid arrest, by warning them before raids so that they can leave the building, while the sex-workers are advised to put vermilion in the parting of their hair and pose as wives of local men (Joarder 1985: 106). If no brothel-keeper is present, then the women can argue that they are operating independently and no crime is being committed. It should be remembered that money changes hands during these raids.

The study by Joarder is rather dated but he seems to have had a knack for catching policemen off their guard. He cites the following comment made by a policeman:

> We must not disturb each other. For the sake of the law we are bound to do our duty, but at the same time we must think about them. That is why before a combing operation we inform them in advance, at least half an hour before. We have suggested some procedures to them so that they can escape the related laws. If they can run their business smoothly, only then can we get our *hafta* [cut, or weekly payment]. Our principle is to 'live and let

live', so that both of us can live without disturbing each other. But for this, they must give us more, because the new act has come and this is why we are taking much trouble to protect them' (Joarder 1985: 186).

Knowing that their seniors and the public tolerate the sex industry, it must be easy for the junior police to collaborate with such ease.

Police harassment is cited as a major problem of the Calcutta sex-workers along with harassment from babus, landlords and local anti-socials. In most red-light areas, except those where the women are well-organized, the police are known to visit regularly for extorting money. Mass arrests are often made, primarily of the sex-workers but also of clients. Although very few charges are actually brought after these mass arrests, money changes hands. We have spoken to senior policemen who say that the facilities in the government remand homes are so bad that arresting the women and sending them there achieves nothing, especially as it is well known that they will soon be released. The senior policemen who do want to help the women feel at a loss and several have tentatively suggested to us that the sex trade should be legalized.

A Calcutta sex-worker has told us that the only difference between the police and other clients is that the police do not pay. Instead, it is they who are paid. The hafta appears to be an accepted and commonplace feature of the sex industry. Many women from a particular red-light area have told us that they regularly pay Rs.50 to the police whenever there is a raid. In a group meeting with residents we discussed how often the police come, how many women have to pay them, and calculated that the local police station covering that area is making an annual of Rs.30,00,000 from this extortion; from one red-light area alone.[3] They either take the women to the police station, or when the police find them with a customer or soliciting for a customer, they remove the client and then return for their money. Most of the women do not know what is legal or illegal about their trade, nor about police procedures for warrants and fines, and so they are unable to stand up to the police.

We have cited two cases in this book (one of trafficking, the other of violent assault) where the police registered false, petty charges when serious crimes against women had been committed. This appears to be common practice. The evidence seems to imply that police are reducing the charges to minor crimes so that the organizers of the sex trade are let off lightly. Others who are involved are the *muhuris* or freelance law clerks who loiter around the police stations, waiting for people to be brought in after raids or arrests. Although muhuris can legitimately assist with bail arrangements for a fee, more often than not they assist with a person's release through an informal system. In the police station itself they are known to take money from the sex-workers and arrange for them to be released almost immediately, without having seen a magistrate or having applied for bail. They are not asked to return to the police station or the court. In these cases the muhuris are in league with the police to take money from the accused, which is usually direct pocket-money for the officials concerned. While the standard experience of sex-workers is to be taken to a police station, pay some money, and then be released, there is no legitimate legal procedure for such cases, as the law demands that arrested people should be brought before a magistrate within 24 hours of arrest, and they should on no occasion pay any money in the police station itself.

Residents of red-light areas have revealed the extent of the police harassment they face. We have learnt a lot from a man in one of Calcutta's largest red-light areas who runs a liquor shop. As the whole area is a hive of criminal activity, the local police allegedly make a killing on the money they take to turn a blind eye. Most liquor shops are illegal because licences take years to be issued; if you are lucky enough to get one at all. Two policemen work at the check-post in shifts, and demand a total of ten rupees each per day from the local people who are involved in various illegal activities. If the people do not pay up they are harassed and threatened by the police. The liquor shop owner himself pays a monthly sum from his profits on top of his daily amount. We have been told that just one liquor shop pays Rs.1,700 monthly to the local police. The money extorted from pimps and mashis who operate the chukri system in the area is added on to the sex-worker's debt which she will have to repay. A posting to a red-light area can be highly lucrative for policemen, more so because their seniors generally do not like to visit these areas and will leave them alone.

We know of a case where a woman was sent back into the sex trade by the police. This woman had been working as a sex-worker under the chukri system. She wanted to leave the profession but had no idea where to go, so she went straight to the local police station asking them to help her find shelter. Legally the police should have arranged for her to stay in a government home for rehabilitation. Instead, they returned her, against her will, to the mashi from whom she had just fled. In many meetings—formal and informal—whenever we have discussed who harasses the women the most, sex-workers say that it is the police, and they usually feel that it is pointless complaining against them. The reality is that the police rarely help those women who want to leave the sex trade, although there is a specific provision in PITA for girls and women who are being detained against their will to contact a magistrate directly for their rescue.

Calcutta's red-light areas are highly organized politically. Areas are represented by municipal councillors who are elected by the residents. The councillor represents a certain political party and guarantees votes for the party by cultivating and nurturing local vested interests. The financial gains from the sex trade, gambling and liquor are major interests in these areas and despite being illegal, they are usually actively supported by the councillors. The politicization of the police or at least their inability to interfere in political conflicts means that they are unable to act against the interests of powerful local leaders. We met with a notorious councillor to discuss our work. His ward covers a red-light area and a sex-workers' receiving centre, and he told us that while he would permit us to carry on our work, he would give us no active support. He told us directly that if we experienced any trouble during the course of our work we should not bother to inform him. It is a well-known fact that members of this councillor's family are directly involved in the sex trade. After six months of our involvement in the area, once we had managed to establish a presence despite his warnings, he came forward to support us.

A SEARCH FOR ALTERNATIVES

An alternative to the existing situation with the law and the police is obviously needed. Not only in India, but also in many countries of the world sex-workers have ranked legal problems among their most significant problems. The International Committee for Prostitute's Rights (ICPR) in the eighties expressed a firm position on legal issues. They argued for the right to work as a sex-worker without coercion and violence, particularly emphasizing stigmatization as an important problem. ICPR called for legal measures to protect their human right to freedom from racism, violence, coercion, child labour and rape, and for legal measures to protect them from these abuses. These demands were made at two regional conferences: in Amsterdam in 1985, and in Brussels in 1986. The majority of the sex-workers present were from Western countries. A regional Asian conference—the Consultation of Prostituted Women and Concerned Activists in Manila—followed in 1988. The sex-workers stated their main problems in order of importance, and ranked the lack of legal protection as their second most important problem, alongside lack of other economic opportunities, and after stigmatization (Van der Vleuten 1993: 41).

Clearly legislation and its implementation are failing to prevent trafficking or to stop excesses of exploitation within the sex industry. On the contrary, the industry continues to thrive while many Calcutta sex-workers say that police harassment is one of their major problems. For any significant improvement, the two issues must be tackled separately. One issue is changing the law itself. For this it is necessary to explore whether legalization or prohibition would be in the best interests of the sex-workers in India, or whether toleration should continue, but with some reforms. The second issue is that whatever the law says on prostitution, the misuse of power within the police force has to be tackled separately.

Legalization

Legalization has proved to be an ineffective way of tackling trafficking and exploitation in other countries where the registered prostitutes are always fewer in number to the unregistered ones. Ironically, when legalization is implemented in a country where sex-work is still stigmatized, it merely pushes a large section of the sex trade underground. Women do not want to be publicly stamped as sex-workers or forced to have medical check-ups. A black economy of trade in women usually continues alongside the registered sector, and the exploitation of these women is often worse than under toleration laws. This was the case in Calcutta at the end of the nineteenth century when the registered women could be forcibly sent to 'lock' hospitals and were subjected to humiliating medical examinations by male doctors. Many chose to remain outside the law rather than register themselves. In India today legalization could simply give the state more power to interfere in the lives of the women. Introducing government bureaucracy in India simply opens up more opportunities for bribes and extortion. In addition, it would be near impossible to find sensitive administrators to handle the registration process. Publicly identified sex-workers would be extremely vulnerable to abuse and extortion from administrators with whom they would have to make contact, as they would be identified and abused as public women. Insensitive handling of registration and enforced medical check-ups would no doubt push the trade underground, where a parallel and worse situation could exist. Underground sex-workers in a legalized system would have fewer rights than sex-workers have at present under the toleration system.

Legal recognition is one of the demands of the Mahila Samanyaya Committees, the organized groups of sex-workers emerging in Calcutta under the guidance of the AIIH&PH (Singh 1995: 36). In April 1996, the first ever convention of sex-workers in India was held to discuss legal issues. Sex-workers were drawn to it from all over India as well as from Bangladesh and Nepal. The Mahila Samanyaya Committees demanded the scrapping of PITA and the establishment of a board to regulate the entry of new girls into the profession and to control development activities in the red-light areas. The board would comprise of sex-workers as a first step towards self-regulation. This is in line with the World Charter for Prostitutes Rights developed at the First World Whores Congress in Amsterdam in 1985 that demanded decriminalization and the setting up of a committee of sex-workers and supporters for the protection of their rights and for addressing their complaints. The demands made at the Calcutta convention by and large received support from other sex-workers, though the details of the proposed board are yet to be worked out. What is clear is that a strong movement is emerging where sex-workers are demanding the end of police control of red-light areas and their right to legal equality with other workers in the informal sector in India. They are also demanding rights and protection for their children.

Most sex-workers we have worked with, particularly during legal workshops, have reacted favourably to the idea of legalizing sex-work, and this has been strongly linked to the desire to eliminate police harassment and to gain more dignity as a sex-worker. The advantage of a legal system would be to reduce harassment from police, abuse from clients, pimps and landlords, and to stop forced trafficking. But since so much of the sex trade in India is about coercion and the lack of choice, would it work to introduce an artificial element of legitimacy to the organizers of the trade? It is unlikely that legalization alone would change the face of the sex trade to a more acceptable one; unless sex-workers and their supporters can exert enough pressure, the abuse would continue with increased state patronage. Currently, sex-workers are only legally harassed when they are soliciting or practising in or near a public place, when they are denied tenancy rights, or removed at the request of a magistrate. It would be beneficial to remove these clauses from the existing laws. This can be done as effectively under the toleration system and need not be accompanied by registration.

Many women's groups abroad are generally against legalization of the sex industry because it is perceived as supporting an attitude to women's bodies that degrades and controls their sexuality, while furthering the myth that male sexuality is uncontrollable and needs to be expressed in a situation devoid of anything other than purely physical intimacy. It is these same images of male and female sexuality that may lead to violence against women, rape and degrading pornography. Within a strongly patriarchal society such as India where women do not generally come into the sex trade as a matter of free choice, legalization would certainly seem to institutionalize and legitimize the existing gender inequalities. It would also be incongruous and hypocritical in a society that simultaneously promotes strong traditional 'family values' in its family laws. As long as women remain socially disadvantaged and continue to join the sex trade as a result of coercion and lack of alternative opportunities, legalizing sex-work would indicate an acceptance of the existing system.

Prohibition

This approach attempts to eliminate the sex trade by making it totally illegal. This is unlikely to be effective in India as it is tackling the symptoms rather than the causes. This approach tends to result in further isolation of the sex-workers as it simply pushes them underground where the abuse and exploitation is likely to be even worse. What would the thousands of women do if they were suddenly not allowed to practise their trade and earn a living? The state could not possibly find alternative employment for them, nor for the hundreds of new girls who join the trade every month. The condition of the state rehabilitation homes is so appalling that any woman would rather work underground than have to live in them. Because the clients' demand for sex-workers would still exist, prices would rise, and women would be prepared to take additional risks of working underground because of the enhanced financial compensation. Most of the exploitative aspects of the sex trade are already illegal, and yet they continue. Prohibition also denies the women a voice in any debate on the issue of prostitution because it does not see them as worthy discussion partners, but as criminals. As part of a longer term strategy for change, though, many feminists support the prohibition of the sex industry through criminalization of the whole trade, including criminalizing the sex-workers and the clients.

Toleration

Given the existing system, almost by default, the de-criminalization of sex-work seems to be the most acceptable approach for India right now. Some reforms would make it more acceptable. It should not be illegal for a sex-worker to solicit in or near a public place, as this is essential to her trade, and helps her to be independent of pimps. (The IPC law on 'public nuisance' could still be applied in case any soliciting was unusually offensive to others.) The law which criminalizes her for practising near a public place should be clarified, as at present it could include servicing clients in a room which is 200 metres away from a road, although in itself it is not really a public place. Living off the earnings of a sex-worker should not always be a crime as this extends to family and babus who may not be extorting money, but may be the sex-worker's legitimate dependents. There is also no reason why, under the present toleration system, clients cannot be penalized for refusing to wear a condom, or for refusing to pay. What is of primary importance is that sex-workers should have the right to legal protection. For example, they should be able to organize on the basis of their profession, make charges against clients or pimps who abuse them, and feel safe to report trafficking to the authorities and act as witnesses against those who have abused them. The legal loopholes which allow traffickers to evade charges need to be tightened.

Such reforms would need extensive debate and consultation with activists and the sex-workers themselves. Dealing with police harassment and abuse of powers separately, we see that support at the most senior levels is essential. Awareness among senior police officers on the ground is badly needed to sensitize them to issues concerning existing legislation. Until the sex-workers can rely on the police and the courts to protect them, instead of contributing to their exploitation, the present hardships are likely to continue, whatever the legal system.

Achieving legal reforms and working to change the role and the attitude of the police will take time. Meanwhile, we need to interpret the existing laws in favour of the sex-workers as much as possible. For example, contradictory laws on tenancy rights can be exploited as in the recent eviction case. If the sex-workers are aware that the laws are not at all intended to hit hardest at them but at the organizers of the trade, at least not in theory, and that they are entitled to certain basic rights as citizens, they can use this to their advantage when fighting for their constitutional rights. What also needs to be emphasized is that the police can be challenged when they themselves do not work within legal constraints.

NOTES

1. Figures from the Immoral Traffic Department, Lalbazar Police Headquarters, Calcutta.
2. Ration cards permit a city dweller to buy rice, wheat and certain other foodstuffs at a subsidized rate from special shops. Possessing a ration card usually validates the person's bonafides in a society that does not have a general system of identity cards.
3. One lakh = 100,000. In usage the comma appears after the number '1' to indicate it is one lakh.

CHAPTER 4

Health and Violence

HEALTH PROBLEMS FACED by any worker in the informal sector can be the beginning of a downward spiral. For sex-workers too, good health is crucial for their work; ill-health can lead to loss of income, expenditure on treatment, loss of regular customers, indebtedness, and then further ill-health because of overwork and inadequate nourishment as they attempt to regain their previous financial position.

While discussing health issues, we have deliberately attempted to present the wide range of health problems that confront sex-workers. This is to redress the balance: at present many NGOs begin working on sexual health issues with sex-workers because of the high profile of the HIV/AIDS epidemic that has translated into large amounts of funding for sexual health projects in red-light areas. The importance of need-based programmes is often overlooked, while many health programmes are based on simple baseline surveys that only cover issues that are already known to the surveyors. They therefore cover existing prejudices while missing out on some other real problems. Interventions often focus overwhelmingly on HIV/AIDS while neglecting other issues. While we acknowledge the urgency of fighting HIV/AIDS at all levels, we also believe that a broader understanding of the sex-workers' other problems and needs, including other health needs, will lead to a more effective and sensitive fight against HIV/AIDS.

GENERAL HEALTH

Clearly from the sex-workers' point of view, sexually transmitted diseases (STDs) are a genuine problem because they are at risk of being infected by clients or babus. They do not, however, usually prioritize STDs as their main health problem. For example, at a meeting of Kalighat sex-workers, malaria, gastric problems, pelvic inflammatory diseases, wounds and cuts from violence and dysentery were all mentioned as major problems, and were ranked as more important than STDs. A wide range of other health problems are faced as a result of their environment, profession, low economic status and their vulnerability to abuse.

Common ailments among sex-workers are due to a lifestyle that involves irregular hours, eating food cooked outside in unhygienic conditions, drinking alcohol with clients, and living in overcrowded places where infections, water-borne diseases and mosquitoes thrive. Malaria, tuberculosis, gastric disorders, skin infections and dysentery are some of the preventable illnesses faced by residents of the red-light areas. Minor sex-workers face additional health problems, and are less likely to be properly treated because of the fear of their profession being discovered. Health problems are aggravated among elderly sex-workers who are likely to have a low income and may therefore be weaker through malnourishment.

The work and lifestyle take their toll on the women's mental health, and their psychological problems and low self-esteem are expressed in acts of self-mutilation such as scarring their own arms with knives, alcohol addiction and tolerance of violent relationships, and occasionally violent behaviour. Low self-esteem often puts the sex-workers in a cycle of violence and abuse. Alcoholism is an occupational hazard as many clients demand that they drink together as part of a visit. The AIIH&PH survey of 1993 found that 69 percent of clients consumed alcohol in the company of sex-workers (Singh 1995: 14). Alcohol interferes with some medication and aggravates some illnesses. Women fear that pills—including contraceptive pills—interact with or are made ineffective by alcohol, and they may not take pills and alcohol together. Also, they are less likely to take pills regularly or use condoms after drinking.

TREATMENT

The health services that are available are diverse, and include government and private hospitals and clinics as well as allopathic and many non-allopathic private practitioners. Government health-care is free but the standards of service and care are low. Sex-workers who can afford it prefer to avail of more efficient and higher standards of care from private practitioners. Quacks, under-qualified practitioners and unlicensed abortionists practise near red-light areas. A wide range of different belief systems are catered to and exist alongside one another: ayurvedic, homeopathic, allopathic and herbal.

Despite free medical care being available in government hospitals and clinics, most sex-workers say they would rather pay the Rs.15-30 fee for a private consultation to avoid travelling, long waits and the unpleasant atmosphere of government facilities. Private doctors are more convenient as they are close by and can usually see a patient immediately. Private nursing homes are also preferred if the woman has enough money, but those on a lower income, and especially elderly sex-workers, have to make do with government hospitals. Private doctors have a tendency to over-prescribe and to prescribe unnecessary drugs and tonics, partly in response to the patients' unrealistically high expectations. Private doctors are competing against each other and so they resort to popularizing their work by prescribing unnecessary injections or more expensive broad-range or brand name drugs. As a result, treatment is often more costly than is absolutely necessary.

Private medical facilities abound in or near most of Calcutta's red-light areas. Despite this, many well-meaning organizations start replica facilities that may be different only in that they are free or subsidized. Some organizations are able to give out free medicines that are received as samples from doctors. The value of these efforts is doubtful as lack of money for treatment is not necessarily the most urgent health-related problem.

Compounders also operate as 'doctors' in the red-light areas,[1] prescribing and selling medicines directly to the patient, supplying loose and unpackaged tablets and giving verbal instructions. Although compounders are popular for minor illnesses because the doctor's fees can be avoided, their unqualified diagnosis is dubious and based only on a verbal description of symptoms. Patients are not told the name of the medicines they are prescribed. We know of one such compounder who is very popular among residents of a red-light area that is close to a large canal where mosquitoes breed and spread malaria. Compounders are also popular for giving injections such as penicillin for STDs. Irrational prescriptions from doctors and ad hoc treatment from compounders can exacerbate health problems. For example, not taking a full course of antibiotics can create resistance and can lead to chronic infections. This is a problem that sex-workers share with the general population. Another complicating factor is that the sex-workers do not always decide independently where and when to go for their treatment or for abortions. Mashis and babus have an interest in the women's health and finances and so they are often over-involved in these decisions.

Abortions

Self-treatments vary according to the traditions of the women's original villages. Informal use of safe herbal remedies is an inherited tradition. Nowdays, some people are manipulating this tradition for their own livelihood and the remedies are no longer harmless. Indrani Sinha met a woman, Mariam, who makes a living as a herbalist. She saw her advertisement—a fly-poster on a lamp post offering cures for missed periods—and went along to see her. This woman specializes in herbs for STDs and performs abortions using roots. Her method is very popular as clients can take the medicine in the privacy of their own homes; her remedies are also very cheap. Knowing a woman who had used roots for an abortion and had been very ill afterwards, Indrani asked her about the safety of her methods. She replied defensively that any accidents that occur are not due to her medicine but due to weakness or anaemia of the patients. 'It is mostly fate,' she said. Mariam is never bothered by the police, even though her address is given on the fly-poster. 'There is always a way out with the police,' she said with a smile. She believes she is a true friend of society, helping so many wronged women and young girls.

Doctors who perform abortions can easily take advantage

of the women's need for privacy and their desire for quick, low-cost treatment. For anonymity, sex-workers frequently go outside their local area for both STD treatment and abortions—however, this means that the practitioner also remains anonymous to others and difficult to trace in the event of any 'mishap'. Abortion clinics even send touts to government hospitals to bring women for private terminations, persuading them that their service will be quicker and easier.

Indrani Sinha visited a doctor on the outskirts of Calcutta who performs two to three abortions a day for sixteen to twenty days a month. He claimed to be licensed but could not produce the certificate that would prove that he is qualified and equipped to conduct abortions. This man was almost sixty years old and had two medically untrained but experienced female assistants. The place was tiny with one bed, two stirrups and a suction machine. It was dirty with no running water, there was an open container of surgical instruments among the things littered around. The 'operation room' was partitioned from the waiting bench by a filthy curtain. Any case needing blood transfusion was sent to the hospital. The doctor said: 'I am saving stupid girls who fall prey to the horrible lust of men.' When asked if there had been any deaths, he kept quiet and shook his head. But the assistants spoke up when alone. They said that there was one death from bleeding a month before—the parents had reported it later. They were raided once by the police over the death of another girl. 'The doctor managed to sort it out as he also belongs to a political party and got the help of the local thugs.' A minimum of Rs.150 is charged per client, but this fee is decided after seeing the economic status of the patient. The assistants said they were paid Rs.100 per month for a four-hour day.

It is impossible to estimate the number of sex-workers who actually die from unsafe abortions. In addition, survivors can suffer haemorrhage, infections, abdominal and intestinal perforation, kidney failure, and permanent infertility.

SEXUAL HEALTH

A common sexual health problem among sex-workers is pelvic inflammatory disease (PID), where infection causes acute pain in the lower abdominal area. Infection of the pelvic area is common and can cause blockages and cysts of the fallopian tubes. Acute pelvic inflammatory disease can cause internal scarring and is related to the infertility problems of sex-workers. This is often described by them in terms of 'the *nari* having shifted'. Many women believe that the body is internally made up of channels known as nari through which vital fluids and energy travel. Sudden jolts such as during painful intercourse can cause the reproductive nari to shift, resulting in pain and swelling. The concept of the nari is central to ayurvedic beliefs, and accepted by the sex-workers. The treatment preferred by many of the women is well known by ayurvedic practitioners.

Some sex-workers are treated at home for PID—an elderly woman will twist the cervix and massage the stomach, or a wick will be burnt over the stomach in traditional ayurvedic style. Other patients visit private doctors who prescribe antibiotics and/or painkillers. Lower abdominal pain is well known among doctors in the red-light areas as a common health hazard of sex-work. There is a 'doctor' who is very popular among the sex-workers in various red-light areas who go to him for treatment. We know that several women from Kalighat and Sonagachhi travel to his clinic in Kidderpore where he performs a quick internal examination and then sells them loose, unwrapped tablets, telling them he has 'put the nari back in place'. It is not widely understood by most sex-workers that these lower abdominal pains are caused by infections and can be prevented by condom use, and there is a need to create more awareness among sex-workers and health workers.[2] Health workers who do attempt to tackle this complaint need to respect the women's own concepts of their bodies, understanding that their ideas are not necessarily wrong but are drawn from a different belief system.

Infertility and miscarriages are a problem faced by many sex-workers. These can be caused by internal scarring, by frequent or improperly conducted abortions, or by untreated STDs. Given that many sex-workers want children and look to them for security in old age, infertility and miscarriages are a high-priority health problem.

Contraception

Contraception is an important health issue for any sexually active woman, and more so for commercial sex-workers. While natural methods or male vasectomy are not options for sex-workers, all other available methods are used: female sterilization, the pill and condoms, with abortion frequently resorted to for unwanted pregnancies. A recent study in one red-light area of Calcutta has shown that sterilization and repeated abortions are the two most common methods of preventing pregnancies among sex-workers (Evans 1995). Another study showed that the pill is the most common form of regular contraception among sex-workers in Sonagachhi (13.6%) followed by ligation (11.6%). On the whole 45 percent of the women were found to be taking precautions against pregnancy (AIIH&PH 1992).

None of the available contraceptive methods are satisfactory. Many women are suspicious of long-term medication and its side-effects, and see the pill as some kind of medication. They may take it only on days when they have sex, or may stop it when they have to take other medicines. The misuse is aggravated because it is usually bought over the counter and not prescribed by doctors who could give information about its use. As stated earlier, many women who are aware of the need to take it regularly forget on nights when they drink a lot of alcohol, or worry that the pill, like antibiotics, will not mix well with alcohol. The IUD (intrauterine device, also known as the Copper T in India because of its shape) is not safe for sex-workers because of the high risk of infections from clients. It is also commonly believed to cause ulcers which are linked to cancer, and so again there is suspicion. Some sex-workers have said that customers can feel the IUD.

Female sterilization is very common, and many women settle for it after trying other options, but it is associated with many post-operative problems. Sex-workers told us that abdominal pains and infections occurred after sterilizations. This could be because they may be doing heavy work too soon after the operation, or because they have caught infections. Even if the problems are not actually caused by the operation, it is important to note that the women are very conscious and aware of any possible complications. Abortion is frequently resorted to, although, as described earlier, private abortionists have been known to perform dangerous operations in unhygienic surroundings with inadequate backup support in case of complications. The women's health suffers in the long term from too many abortions, and there is an added risk of becoming infertile. Doctors are not in the habit of giving contraceptive advice after abortions and so the cause of the first unwanted pregnancy can easily be repeated. It is also reported that high dose hormone pills are bought over the counter to induce bleeding if a pregnancy is suspected, but these are highly risky and may not result in an abortion.

Fears and suspicions about the various contraceptive methods are common among the women and any bad experience quickly becomes common knowledge. For example, Sanlaap was inundated with requests for ECGs after a rumour spread around Kalighat about the possible side-effects of the pill. Similarly, we know of a sex-worker in another red-light area who became pregnant after a ligation. This is a very small area where the news spread quickly to all the residents, and afterwards the other women of the area totally lost faith in this method.

Given the dearth of safe and acceptable contraceptives for women, what emerges is that the condom is highly important as a contraceptive, and not only for HIV prevention. However, there are many problems associated with using condoms. Condoms require cooperation from clients and babus, and take up precious time to discuss, fit and use. The whole process becomes more time-consuming as men take longer to ejaculate when using a condom. Some women working in the aadhiya system just do not have the time to make their clients use the condom as other women are waiting to use the beds. The mashis also discourage its use because the more clients the sex-workers see, the more money the mashis make. Some customers are willing and will even bring their own condoms, but others are not interested and will get angry when the women bring up the subject. Regular 'fixed' clients who have become friends usually object when the women suggest a condom if they have not used one before. Live-in babus are even more difficult to convince, although the women know that the babus are probably unfaithful to them and are very much aware of

the need for protection even within their long-term relationships. A survey by AIIH&PH found that less than 5 percent of
the babus regularly used condoms with their partners; 72.7
percent had never used condoms; and 22.7 percent used them
frequently (Singh 1995: 14).

These problems with condom-use are easier to overcome in
small red-light areas where the women are more able to organize and take decisions independently of mashis and babus.
For example, in Kalighat in 1994 it was estimated that 80
percent of the women were regularly using condoms with their
one-off clients. The other 20 percent were using them irregu-
larly. This achievement is attributed to the AIIH&PH project.
There are several factors, however, that have helped the project to be such a success in this area. The women are working
independently without mashis and simply with fixed rents to
pay. The area is relatively small, with five to six hundred
women practising there. A history of strong leadership and of
success in disputes with police and others has given the
women a sense of confidence that empowers them to negotiate
condom-use. In the small community where the residents are
all known to each other and to the AIIH&PH peer educators, it
has been easier to spread awareness and to encourage the
women to help each other out when they need to refuse customers. They have decided first to take the money from the
clients and then to persuade them to use condoms, so either
way they get to keep the money. The 20 percent who continue
to have sex with one-off clients without condoms are those
with special problems such as alcoholism, which also some-
what alienates them from the others, or those in financial need
such as the elderly women who will quietly take the risks in
order to get more customers.

The 1993 AIIH&PH statistics from the Calcutta red-light areas have shown that women who use fewer condoms with clients are in the lowest income group, but this figure is not
significantly different from the data on condom-use for middle
and higher income sex-workers (Singh 1995: 17). It may be
that customers who pay more believe that they are entitled
to condom-free sex, or that even the high income women are
not earning enough to be able to refuse customers who do not
wear condoms.

Sexually Transmitted Diseases

Many people feel that sexually transmitted diseases (STDs) are the major health problems faced by sex-workers. STDs are usually the first thing that comes to mind whenever the sex industry is mentioned to outsiders. Many people who ask about the work of Sanlaap assume that we are working on the issue of HIV/AIDS, and the first question is usually about HIV prevalence in the red-light areas. The first legislation ever passed in India on the sex trade was the Contagious Diseases Act. Professionals have sometimes argued for legalization of the sex industry, not out of concern for the sex-worker's own health, but in order to enforce medical check-ups for the purpose of controlling STDs: representatives of the Maharashtra and the Karnataka state governments as well as official bodies have discussed legalization primarily for the sake of public health (D'Cunha 1991: 103). No health authorities, to our knowledge, have thought about legalizing the sex industry because it might help to tackle the various other health problems of the sex-workers themselves. The ghettoization of sex-workers makes them an easier target than men for health surveys that focus on STDs, generating statistics that reinforce and perpetuate the stereotype of sex-workers as dirty and diseased. A survey among truck drivers in West Bengal found that 60 percent of the respondents cited fear of illness as the main factor for reducing the number of visits to sex-workers (Society for Research on Haemotology and Blood Transfusion 1993).

Sexually transmitted diseases are actually highest among younger sex-workers and, once a woman has experienced STDs she is more careful in future and quickly seeks treatment. Sex-workers actually have their own methods for identifying STDs in their customers, for example, looking for sores or putting some lime juice on their hands when touching a man's penis to see if he winces. They also discretely examine a man's undergarments for discharge, and are suspicious of men who insist on having sex in the dark. If they do discover signs of a STD in a client they can refuse to have sex with him, persuade him to use a condom, or just give him manual stimulation. Some women are quite sympathetic to these men and do what they can to persuade them to go for treatment.

HIV *and* AIDS

The threat of HIV worldwide has resulted in research and action in the red-light areas in India, as more and more HIV-related funds have poured into the country. According to 1995 data of the National AIDS Control Organization (NACO), there were 7.79 HIV cases in India per 1,000 persons screened; 21,564 HIV cases detected; and 2,109 cases of AIDS detected (529 female, 1,580 male). In West Bengal 39 AIDS cases have been detected, while there have been 252 HIV cases.

The prevalence of HIV and AIDS is currently low in Calcutta compared to other Indian cities. In the city's red-light areas where the government HIV Intervention Programme is working, a survey was conducted with 612 women in November-December 1993. Out of these, 607 serum samples were tested and seven (1.15%) were found to be HIV-positive with the Western Blot test (AIIH&PH, Singh 1995: 18). The intervention projects being implemented by the government and NGOs to reduce the risks of infection seem to have had some impact already. Health interventions that target sex-workers have overwhelmingly focused on condom use, combining dissemination of information with condom distribution. The AIIH&PH is implementing the largest STD/HIV intervention programme in West Bengal, working through clinics and peer educators. They have been largely successful in creating awareness about STDs and HIV and the need for condoms, although the social problems surrounding condom-use remain.

HIV has brought red-light areas into the limelight as high-risk areas, but the surge of funds has very specific epidemiological goals that do not match with the perceived needs of the sex-workers. More tangible and visible benefits have been the jobs for peer educators and related employees that have brought security and exposure to new experiences, people and places and dignity to many of the residents.

The danger is that in the race to control the epidemic women in high-risk groups can easily become scapegoats. For example, in 1994 a Calcutta NGO allegedly forced blood tests on sex-workers in the presence of the police as part of a survey to support a HIV project application. This was immediately taken up by NGOs and sex-workers who publicly condemned the action. Panic, ignorance and a deluge of funds to run HIV-related programmes has led to such violations of human rights. Enforced testing and insensitive handling of HIV cases have sent people with HIV underground. Complex issues such as how to reach clients have not been resolved. We can ask ourselves why enforced testing of clients has never occurred.

Sex-workers have also been used for illegal vaccine trials. In March 1994, doctors and government officials of the Indian Health Organization (IHO), along with two American doctors, conducted trials of a Bovine Immuno-Deficiency Virus vaccine on four Calcutta sex-workers. The trials were illegal as the women had not consented, the vaccines had not been tested on animals, and the women were not monitored and examined afterwards (*The Asian Age*, 10 November 1995). The work of AIIH&PH in the Calcutta red-light areas has brought about more awareness and sensitivity to these issues but many needs remain, such as counselling people with HIV, particularly HIV-positive sex-workers who have no alternative employment options and who need to remain in contact with the health services and counsellors for the sake of their own health and their clients.

What is crucial to HIV prevention in the sex industry is that clients who refuse to practise safe sex and wear condoms should be taken to task and prevented from having sex with sex-workers. Sex-workers themselves are often not in a financial position to refuse these customers, and those who are financially worse off will have to take the risks. The only situation where unsafe clients will be refused is if sex-workers know that no other sex-worker will do business with those men. The women in each area have to organize themselves for their own safety so that clients will have no choice but to practise safe sex. As condoms require client cooperation the education of clients is essential. As for the women, they have to have information and tools for self-protection, the main tool being the power to say no to high risk clients. Supportive legal options could also be explored. For example, in the state of Nevada in the USA a client can be jailed if he refuses to wear a condom and forces himself on a sex-worker (*The Illustrated Weekly of India*, 25 April 1992).

The scapegoating of sex-workers for HIV transmission has

another danger over and above the possible impact on the women themselves. Targetting high-risk groups can create a sense of invulnerability among the general population, who identify HIV with groups rather than behaviours. It is essential to ensure that vulnerable groups are targetted for their own sake and that the general population is aware that they themselves are at risk from unsafe behaviour and not from identified groups.

HEALTH PROBLEMS OF MINORS

The Indian Health Organization's definition of a minor from a medical perspective is any person below the age of eighteen. Using this definition the IHO has estimated that 20 percent of all sex-workers in India are minors. We estimate a similar proportion in Calcutta. We are aware of very young girls working in many of the Calcutta red-light areas, and in three areas in particular. During 1989, 431 minors were arrested under the Immoral Traffic in Persons (Prevention) Act—all were girls. Of the 575 rape cases reported in West Bengal, 217 were of children below the age of sixteen (Ministry of Home Affairs, 1989). It is very difficult to collect accurate figures of minors who are working in the red-light areas or of rape. The police headquarters at Lalbazar have informed us that from April 1995 to March 1996, there were 446 arrests under the IPC of which 52 were rape cases. None of the agents has been charge-sheeted. The police have cautioned that this information is not complete.

In addition to the health problems already mentioned, minors who are not fully developed physically face problems as a result of sexual activity. It is reported from various sources in the red-light areas that the demand for child sex-workers is increasing, particularly as they are seen to be freer of STDs than older sex-workers. Notwithstanding the mental strain, the physical effects of sexual abuse on minors are horrific. From doctors we received accounts of what both child sex-workers and child victims of non-commercial sex-abuse have suffered: the internal injuries are so severe that repair is difficult; they suffer from rectal fissures, lacerated vaginas, poor sphincter control, foreign bodies in the anus, perforated anal and vaginal walls, chronic choking from gonorrhoeal tonsillitis, and death by asphyxiation. CINI (ASHA) came across a fifteen-year-old girl whose anal muscles were hanging outside her body after repeated anal rape. To make matters worse, the risk of catching HIV is increased in children because of the higher incidence of abrasions and bleeding when sex occurs. In terms of medical care, the child victims of sexual abuse and sex-work are appallingly vulnerable as their pimps are afraid to take them to doctors for fear of being discovered. We surmise that they presumably go untreated or are helped by quacks and home remedies.

The number of clients entertained per day is higher among younger sex-workers because of the higher demand. Studies have shown that the average number of clients per week ranges from twelve to twenty-nine (CINI pilot study 1993) or, for over 60 percent respondents in a study by the AIIH&PH, three to four per day (AIIH&PH 1993). The 1988 Development Dialogue study found fifteen- to nineteen-year-old girls among the most active group serving an average 2.8 customers per day. However these figures generalize across age groups and do not account for seasonal variations such as busy puja or festival times.

VIOLENCE

Violence and the threat of violence affect physical and mental health. The threat of violence from local anti-socials is used against new sex-workers to prevent them from leaving the profession. Unorganized sex-workers are easily controlled in the face of such organized violence. The hoodlums also think they can possess and control women of their choice. They identify new sex-workers whom they want to be with, and decide that they will be their babus even if the women protest. This means they have free access to particular women, who are sometimes even forced to live with them as if they are lovers. In the areas where the women have not been able to organize themselves into groups, these men who are backed up by other local anti-socials have enough support to intimidate the women into accepting these arrangements.

We worked with a case where a sex-worker was beaten up

by hoodlums who wanted her to belong to a man who would have become her babu. She disliked the man and refused to become his partner, and so was beaten up by several men. She was taken to the hospital and the police station, but the police were not interested and simply filed a general diary without doing any investigation. The woman suffered a temporary breakdown after the assault. We know of women who have been forced to give shelter to hoodlums who hide from police or other gangs in their rooms.

Domestic violence is another problem faced by many women living in red-light areas. Many sex-workers and their children come from violent homes, later entering into violent relationships once they are in the sex industry. The majority have babus, many of whom are financially dependent on the sex-workers. Champa is such a woman who has a violent partner. She has a mother and a sister who are both sex-workers. Joining the profession herself, she moved to a different area where she could earn more money. There she had two sons by a local hoodlum who had become her babu. After a quarrel they split up and she moved again to keep out of his way. After some time she met Dilip who ran a paubhaji and bhelpuri stall[3] at the Maidan and also sold illicit liquor. He moved in with her and she had two more sons by him. She continued to work as a sex-worker. Things began to turn sour when the hawkers were removed from a part of the Maidan to build a fountain. All of Dilip's equipment and pots were smashed by the police and he became unemployed. He started drinking throughout the day and then he would come to Champa and start beating her up for money for his drinks. She gave him food but tried to stop him from coming into her room. Now he visits her two or three times a week and threatens or beats her for money. Sometimes he visits late at night, climbs over the wall of the courtyard and enters her room, shouting abusive language if the door is locked. The older children flee and the younger ones cry when he comes—he has also beaten the children in the past.

Champa continues to entertain clients but nowadays takes the risk of operating from outside a public monument that is a tourist attraction, going with rich clients who come in cars. She earns Rs.150-300 per customer, and more if she goes to a hotel with them. The risks are greater but she needs the money, for herself, her sister, her four children and for Dilip's liquor. She is unable to stop the harassment because Dilip leads a group of hoodlums around the monument who could stop her business. Dilip has started earning a little money playing the priest and doing pujas for tourists who come to visit the monument, and she says he also steals. He tried to rape her sister once when he was totally drunk, and was beaten by Champa's neighbours. Champa receives regular counselling from Sanlaap and two of her children attend our creche. She also wants us to counsel Dilip.

Like domestic violence all over the world, in the red-light areas too it is seen as a private issue and outsiders are reluctant to intervene. If they do, they are often disappointed to find that couples later on get back together again. A woman we know requested another to help her throw out her live-in babu after she could bear his abuse no more. They sent him away, but after a few months he was back and living with the same woman. Her friend says she is very disillusioned. 'Women take this abuse because they love their babus and they need that love. They don't report domestic violence to the police. It is a private matter.'

Women tolerate violent relationships for many reasons: lack of alternatives, fear, desire to maintain a stable relationship, need for protection and low self-esteem. If the babus are members of gangs of hoodlums or political groups they often wield considerable power that helps to intimidate the sex-worker into accepting a violent relationship and ensures her silence. Leaving violent men often entails leaving the area completely, and many sex-workers who move from one red-light area to another do so to escape violent relationships.

Many sex-workers have experienced sexual assault from men who think they are always sexually available. Many otherwise intelligent men argue that a sex-worker cannot be raped. Recently we prepared communication materials on the sex-workers' legal rights and a male artist illustrated the procedure that a woman who had been raped should follow with the police. He could not comprehend what we were doing and asked again and again how a sex-worker could possibly be raped. By contrast, when we later discussed rape and the law

with the sex-workers, they knew with absolute clarity that a
sex-worker could be raped, and knew very clearly the difference between consensual, commercial sex and rape. Activist
sex-workers have themselves challenged many cases of rape
or attempted rape. We know about a babu who lived with a
woman, Sandhya, in a Calcutta red-light area. He took a fancy
to Rekha, a sex-worker, but the two women knew each other
and Rekha did not want to entertain him. He kept bothering
her, and one night tried to enter her room. She called for help
and some local activists and NGO volunteers came and removed
him. They roughed him up a little and he now knows that he
will be arrested if he tries to bother her again.

   Although rarely spoken of, most sex-workers have experienced violent inductions into the business. Local hooligans will
want to have sex with new girls as of right, and may do so
in a group, which is in actual fact gang-rape. Those women
who are forced into sex-work might be raped many times before they resign themselves to what is happening and then,
given their powerlessness to refuse, cooperate with what is
seen as consent. Some cooperate from the beginning, knowing
the alternatives. A senior policeman whose area of jurisdiction
covers one of the largest Calcutta red-light areas estimated
that 20 percent of the girls were brought forcibly, and out of
these only 10 percent resist once they are required to start
practising. We cannot interpret lack of resistance as consent,
however, given the pressure many girls are under and the lack
of alternatives once they have been brought to a red-light area.
It is not too far off the mark to talk of sexual abuse and rape
as a daily occurrence that the women, being powerless to resist, have grown used to. Thus faced with regular abuse and
rape, they have decided to try and make some money out of
this situation. 'Consent' is always to be liberally interpreted
in this context, remembering that consent can only be given
in a situation where choices exist. For many women the other
options are so appalling that they have, in fact, resigned themselves to their present situations. Sex-workers have experienced this abuse in many forms and often deeply internalize
a sense of worthlessness after having been treated as a mere
sexual commodity, as less than human. It is not unusual to
find women who have mutilated themselves, for example by

slashing their arms, as a way of expressing self-loathing after experiencing years of abuse from others.

Calcutta sex-workers have generally reported that actual violence from clients is not common. Once they have got over their initiation into the business, their experiences of violence are overwhelmingly from local hooligans and landlords. In a workshop on violence against women, a group of former sex-workers ranked violence and harassment from clients as the least common, after landlords, local anti-socials or hoodlums, babus and the police. As discussed before, the women at risk from customer violence are those who go out of the designated red-light areas—in a car, boat, to a hotel or to the 'khali kuthis' or vacant houses with customers.

A Nepalese woman working in Calcutta was approached by a client. She knew the young man—he was wealthy and came in a car. She agreed to spend the night with him elsewhere and he drove away with her. After some time they reached another suburb of Calcutta where they were joined by three of his friends. She remembers being sexually tortured by them, and then waking up in a government hospital later, covered with slashes. She had been knifed on the neck, chest and face—her arms and hands alone were covered with twenty-three slashes. A nurse warned her that some young men had been hanging around and asking for her, so with the nurse's help she quickly left the hospital and returned to her room. Her room-mates informed our staff and a FIR was lodged with the police. She was treated by a doctor from AIIH&PH.

Soon after, the men returned to her area. She recognized them and mobilized some local activists who managed to catch one of the men and took him to the local police station. The case was referred to the suburb where the original case had been lodged. The following day, however, they learnt that the young man had only been charged with a petty crime and later released on bail. They returned to the police station along with the victim and showed her injuries to the officer-in-charge. After filing a second FIR the man was arrested and charged with attempted murder. The woman has not been able to work since the attack. She is lucky because she lives with two other sex-workers who are very supportive, and her land-lady is also sympathetic. We are helping her out financially until she is able to work again. The main concern is how she will cope with the trauma of returning to work after being almost killed by a client. We repeat that one of the most high-risk activities with clients is going away with them on a two-wheeler or in a car, especially if the car contains several men. Aware of the risks, the women can charge high prices. But we also know of several women who simply refuse to go in cars after having terrible experiences, some of which have left the women with permanent scars from physical abuse, to say nothing of the mental trauma.

Sometimes the police have not only failed to protect the women from violence but have themselves been perpetrators. In 1989 a woman was badly beaten by a policeman from a local police station after he entered her room. The leaders of a local group demonstrated at the police station and demanded to see the officer-in-charge. They took a photograph of the woman who had been assaulted and reported the case. The officer denied that the policeman had entered her room, and defended him by saying that it was the job of the police to deal with 'drunken prostitutes who stand around the lanes'. Eventually he did admit that the incident had taken place in the woman's room, acknowledged the problem and agreed that the police would no longer enter any woman's room in future. There have been no cases of police atrocities against sex-workers in this area since, although they continue to take money from the women in return for policing the area.

Some female residents of these areas are not merely victims but are themselves violent, caught up in the world of addiction and crime. For example, we know of women who get together in groups of four or five to threaten clients to hand over their wallets and valuables. We also know that local anti-socials work together with sex-workers to lure clients into rooms and then rob them. One technique is to promise the client a fifteen- or sixteen-year-old girl who is supposedly hidden in a room, and then take him there simply to rob him.

This discussion of violence has highlighted violence against women because we believe that generally, women as a group are victims of a gender-based violence that is directed by men towards women as an expression of male power over women— a male power that is supported in many other ways by customs, traditions and institutions in this society. We wish to present these cases as part of the phenomenon of violence against women rather than as violence per se. What is apparent in the red-light areas is that violence is a way of life. Sex-workers, by virtue of being women who are in powerless positions relative to men, face a different kind of violence, which reflects the reality of a wider social system over and above the fact that the area is generally violent. Sex-workers are threatened with sexual violence, they face violence at home, and are in a social context where women can rarely fight back. Even where the woman is financially supporting the man, that he is in control is still an issue in the relationship. If in reality he is not, then often his frustration spurs him to use violence to re-establish control. On their part the women in the sex trade have been raised to be married and have learnt and internalized the necessary feminine values that would bring them good husbands. Only later have they learnt to be more aggressive, and have even been caught up in criminal activities. Because of these power issues surrounding violence, we support the recent initiative in a Calcutta red-light area where women and girls are learning karate for self-defence.

NOTES

1. Assistants, sometimes with pharmacological training, often attached to chemists shops.
2. Catrin Evans, personal communication, 1996.
3. Local fast food.

CHAPTER 5

Financial Issues

Mnjths

ONE OF THE myths surrounding the sex trade is that sex-workers have succumbed to the lure of easy money, that they value money over and above their 'honour', and have somehow chosen an easy way out of poverty by selling their bodies. This argument is often used to label the sex-workers as deviant and to justify their stigmatization. This myth carries with it three assumptions. First, that the work is highly lucrative; second, that the work is easy; and, finally, that the sex-workers have chosen their profession freely in the first place. None of these assumptions is true in India.

Uneducated and unskilled women can potentially earn more in sex-work than in many other jobs open to them, but sex-work is far from lucrative. To judge whether the work is easy or not one cannot simply compare selling sex with cleaning other people's houses, or breaking bricks under the sun. Part and parcel of the profession is being cast out by society, having to send one's children away, taking dangerous health risks. It is highly doubtful that the profession is an easy option; rather, it appears to be far from it. It is also the case in India that the majority of sex-workers have not freely chosen this profession, and so the whole concept of options is entirely inappropriate.

The sex industry as a whole is economically significant, although it is totally within the black economy. In 1988 a study by Development Dialogue estimated that the sex industry in

India is a Rs.500 crore business,[1] with at least half of the money going to the organizers rather than to the sex-workers. Out of the eight Calcutta red-light areas covered in the study, they found that the sex-workers themselves were earning 17.5 crore rupees annually, out of which over 8 crore rupees went into the hands of the organizers (Das Gupta 1990: 9). This did not include the money earned by women in the chukri system, the bonded labourers who hand over all that they earn for the organizers, nor the amounts spent indirectly on alcohol, tips, food and so on.

EARNING CAPACITY

The AIIH&PH Intervention Programme has categorized the sex-workers from Sonagachhi according to high-, middle- and low-income groups to give an idea of the kind of earning capacity of individual sex-workers. The women in the high-income bracket earn over Rs.100 per single act with one client (for approximately twenty minutes), the women in the middle bracket charge between Rs.50-100, while the lowest earning group receive less than Rs.50 per single act. Proportionally, the high-income group represents 21.5 percent of women, the middle-income 51.7 percent, and the low-income 26.8 percent (AIIH&PH 1992). Sonagachhi is the only area in Calcutta catering to high-income clients, and other areas would show a higher proportion of middle- and low-income women. For example, the study in Sett Bagan red-light area found that virtually all of the women were in the low-income bracket, charging just Rs.25 or less per customer (Evans 1995: 9).

The variations can be enormous, for example, Rozario's all-India study found the highest charge for a single act was Rs.3,500, the lowest a meagre Rs.2. While it is difficult to calculate approximately how many clients women see per day, the individual incomes of sex-workers for specified time periods have been widely studied, and the results show huge variations from woman to woman, from place to place. The AIIH&PH study in 1992 found that a Calcutta sex-worker's weekly income ranged from the lowest at just below Rs.300 to the highest at just over Rs.5,000. A smaller study by the All Bengal Women's Union (1988) found the range to be much lower, from between Rs.250-750 per month. Our own study among the women with whom we work found that almost 70 percent were earning less than Rs.60 a day, and of these most were earning less than Rs.30 a day. A sex-worker who earns Rs.30 a day makes approximately Rs.750 per month (for 25 working days), a figure that would leave her well below the poverty line.

The amount of money a sex-worker can charge a client varies according to her desirability, her current health status, the area she works in, and the amount of risk she is prepared to take. For example, a low-income sex-worker can earn more by accepting a client who refuses to wear a condom, who wants to take her away in a car or to a hotel. They can also charge more for variations on straight sex—such as oral or anal sex. Young women are generally able to earn more, although older women can also build up a good market if they have fixed clients who give a regular monthly amount. Because new sex-workers are always popular, women move from one red-light area to another now and again, or go to a totally new area (from Calcutta to places such as Orissa, even as far as Bombay) when particularly needy. If they do this during festival times they can earn even more as these are the busiest times. Rates in Bombay are far higher than in Calcutta, so many women are taken there temporarily to bring in more money, although this does not always benefit the workers themselves.

How much of the earnings actually go to the sex-worker depends on the system she works under, whether she works independently, in aadhiya or in chukri, and whether she uses a pimp who takes a cut. The system of using pimps as mediators is not always financially exploitative, as the women can bring in more clients without having to risk arrest by standing on the streets themselves. Some pimps, however, have a great deal of power over the women and extort excessive amounts of money. Some independent sex-workers who choose to use one or several pimps negotiate a percentage per client and give this at the time of receiving the client. Among women working independently, however, there is a general trend of not using pimps. In one red-light area the pimps were thrown out by the women along with others who were seen to be exploiting them, and in another, the system never really

organized system

took on, and the women there solicit independently. Many pimps are simply rickshaw-pullers or men who work at tea-stalls who supplement their income by occasionally sending customers to a sex-worker they know. Young and naive women are sometimes charged as much as a 50-percent cut from pimps, whereas the more experienced women are able to bargain a lower rate. In some areas the rate is fixed by the *dalals*, the local organizers of the sex trade, while in others it is negotiable. At present in Sonagachhi, a local committee exists that organizes and controls sex-workers coming from certain areas of Rajasthan and Uttar Pradesh, and known as the Agrawali community. The committee recruits and controls the pimps who mediate between clients and sex-workers and is also involved in bringing new girls to the area. The women rarely stand on the street but mediate all their work through pimps. The standard rate in Sonagachhi for pimps is 25 percent of the sex-workers earnings (Singh 1995). The Agrawali women have a reputation for attracting regular customers and are in the highest income bracket in Sonagachhi. Many Agrawali women are coming to this red-light area and are threatening the trade of the other sex-workers, mainly the Bengalis, who feel they are being pushed out. The community is taking control of more and more property in the area.

Some fixed clients pay a regular monthly sum to the women. We know of several cases where these fixed clients have expected the women to stop entertaining other clients. One woman receives just Rs.700 a month from her babu and yet he forbids her from seeing other men. She feels very annoyed that he 'behaves like a husband', even though he does not give her enough to support herself and her children.

Expenses are high and often exceed the income, pushing women into debt. Traders going from house to house sell their goods— food, clothes, jewellery—at a mark up, and give easy credit with high interest to sex-workers. Many women are in debt, not only to moneylenders and landlords, but to tailors, clothes sellers, food-stall owners, dispensaries, cigarette stall-owners, as well as police and clerks of the law court.

debt

A high proportion of the sex-workers' earnings goes towards supporting other family members in their villages—their children and their parents. In 1988 Development Dialogue found

that a sex-worker sends on an average Rs.485 per month
(Rs.5,700 annually) to families in rural areas (Das Gupta 1990:
10), and their survey 'indicated that almost every girl had two
or more to feed other than her own children' (Das Gupta,
Ghosh and Das Gupta 1989-1990: 232-243). Some parents who
have put their children into sex-work come to visit regularly
to collect their money. Family responsibilities also include the
dowries for siblings and daughters, and land for families in
rural areas. The kind of temporary relationships the women
enter into with babus often bring an added financial responsibility and an extra mouth to feed, although some babus do
help the women out financially. Other expenses include child-
care, private health-care, and donations to puja committees
and local functions—usually organized by political parties.

PROBLEMS OF OLD AGE

The capacity to earn quick money is offset by the limited number of working years. Older women lose their charm along with
their customers. Between the ages of about thirty-five to forty-
five, the women who do not have babus or children supporting
them have to start looking for alternative sources of income.
Some work is available, such as supervising and caring for children, cooking and cleaning for practising sex-workers. Enter-
prising sex-workers join the ranks of the organizers of the trade
as they get older, working as mashis and bringing in new girls.
Others begin to get involved in small businesses, selling liquor,
tea, paan or bidis. Rozario reports that 'most of the paanwallis
and women beggars in Calcutta are ex-prostitutes' (Rozario
1988: 118). She mentions that others go to temple cities such
as Puri and Benares where they believe it will be easier for
them to live off alms. Women can make a living as sex-workers
until forty-five and even fifty years, although their earnings
peak between eighteen and thirty-five. The older women who
suffer from increased competition from younger girls have to
lower their rates, yet still attract fewer customers.

Fixed babus who pay regular money to their partners are
particularly welcome as old age draws near. This time of dependency comes early for sex-workers. As their income decreases they are first unable to pay their daily rent and will

lose their rooms. They will sleep on a neighbour's verandah or will be given some other shelter by their landladies if they are lucky. After losing their rooms they find that they are no longer given loans, and start depending on others, on charity, eating a few extra chappatis that a neighbour may have cooked or asking for some free food from a store. They might begin working for landladies or younger sex-workers, doing household chores in return for food or a small sum of money.

Many elderly sex-workers are alcoholic. A case in point is Durga, in her seventies, who was once a very popular sex-worker. She sleeps on a friend's verandah. She does housework for a local landlady, washing clothes and utensils and fetching food and liquor from the shops. In return she is given food and about Rs.5 per day. She needs a drink every day, and so sits around near the liquor stall chatting to the women and men who drink there. She asks for a small glassful and usually manages to beg a little. People from the neighbourhood admitted her to Mother Teresa's Home for the Dying and Destitute a number of times, but she usually caused problems because she wanted her daily drink. She has discharged herself a few times, and now when she is taken back even the nuns say there is no point in re-admitting her. It is also difficult for aged sex-workers to adjust to the routines of a home.

As a younger woman Durga had a fixed babu with whom she had a son. The babu took the son away and he is being raised elsewhere, ignorant of who his mother is. She is no longer with this babu but he returns occasionally during pujas and leaves some clothes and money with her. It has been suggested that he pay her a regular pension but he will not commit himself. She seems to be able to manage except when she falls sick. Then she just lies on the lane without proper shelter or care. She is lucky because at least some local residents try and take care of her and help her out when she is ill.

A proposed solution to the problems of elderly sex-workers who have no shelter or source of income is a home specifically for them. A quiet life of dependency in an institution is probably not the most appropriate solution, given that they have been used to leading independent lives. What might be more effective would be employment schemes so that the women can be economically active as long as possible, savings and credit schemes, and provision of community care in old age.

SAVINGS AND CREDIT

Despite a considerable earning capacity, very few sex-workers manage to save. Women who have been in debt spend much of their excess money repaying loans. Gold and silver are bought as savings when money is available. Alternatively, banks and post offices are used, as well as chit funds organized by local groups.[2] While some of these chit funds are legitimate, there have been cases of ones that were set up without licenses and that have collapsed, resulting in large losses. All chit funds that are operated by private companies, are supposed to be licensed by the Reserve Bank of India, but unlicensed chit funds have been promoted in red-light areas. Touts went out to find new members, convincing people that their money would be safe with them, giving official-looking pass-books and managing to gather hundreds of thousands of rupees from individual depositors. These companies would then suddenly fold and the deposits would be lost. One infamous chit fund was the Monali Fund that collapsed, resulting in losses of hundreds of thousands of rupees of sex-workers in the Sonagachhi area. Sex-workers and other residents marched to the police station to lodge a complaint, but they never succeeded in getting their money back. Post office and bank accounts seem to be the safest place for deposits.

Loans are easy to take and are an indispensable system in all the red-light areas. Mashis and landlords offer soft loans, and the repayment is adjusted against the daily rent with interest. Traders also offer loans; 60 percent interest on loans is common (Project Team, AIIH&PH 1996:7). Because most sex-workers are not literate they are vulnerable to financial exploitation when depositing money and taking loans. Some babus cheat young, naive sex-workers of their money. We know of some who have offered to deposit money for their partners, but have pocketed it instead. For example, one man was asked to take some money to pay his daughter's school fees, but he spent it on himself. The mother, a sex-worker, found out when the school told her that the fees were unpaid.

Surprisingly, NGOs in Calcutta have not taken up savings

and credit schemes in red-light areas in a big way, although they could have a significant impact in solving the financial problems of sex-workers, as well as promoting group formation. A recent initiative has been the formation of the Usha Cooperative ('Usha' meaning 'dawn') by sex-workers under the guidance of the AIIH&PH. These cooperatives have begun savings and credit schemes as well as other economic initiatives. The gains of the sex-workers are actually very limited. They do have food, shelter and an income as long as they are lucky enough to remain attractive and healthy. They are often able to support their families as well as raise their children on their earnings. Yet they live in small rooms in dirty, crowded conditions. They share rooms with beds partitioned off by flimsy curtains. They fall into debt to pay for medical expenses for themselves and their families. Their profession both requires and encourages high spending on clothes, make-up, junk jewellery and alcohol. Their goals are short term and savings minimal. In fact, the earning capacity of the women benefits others far in excess of their contribution, and for the sex-workers what is left is a meagre compensation for the work, the risks, and the lifestyle they have to endure.

NOTES

1. One crore rupees = Rs.100 lakhs or 10 million.
2. Chit funds are privately organized savings schemes. Promoters often visit people in their homes to market the fund and take small deposits in return for a *chit*, a receipt or a note.

CHAPTER 6

Working Mothers:
Children and Childcare

WE HAVE MANY identities: as family members, as friends, as colleagues, as consumers. Most of us are not defined by just one aspect of our identity. Yet sex-workers find that their lives are defined so completely by their work that it becomes difficult to imagine them in any other role. In a workshop held in July 1995 to discuss how the law deals with prostitution, participants told us that one of their greatest desires was to be free of the label of 'sex-worker', to have their other roles recognized instead of being forever lost behind that all-consuming label. The stereotypes of sex-workers and mothers would have us believe that the two are mutually exclusive, yet the majority of sex-workers do have children and are skilled parents. A study of sex-workers in Calcutta found that 40 percent of the women had children (AIIH&PH 1992). Sex-workers take on a lot of the responsibility of parenting because most of them, at one time or another, are single parents. Parenting for sex-workers is much more of a challenge than for women in most other professions. First, as single parents, they have to be both father and mother, being the breadwinner in addition to all the traditionally feminine caring roles. Second, the stigma of the sex industry and the environment of the red-light areas strongly influence the lives of the children.

Why do sex-workers choose to have children, and how do they rear them in their non-traditional families? What are the influences on the child growing up in a red-light area and what child-care can be provided? We found that while many women want children, many prefer to send their children away to live with relatives or in schools that provide boarding. Is institutional care a preferred option, or are coping strategies within the community more appropriate?

Maya, for example, joined the profession many years ago, as a young mother and the wife of an alcoholic husband. She says that her first good experience here was giving birth to her second daughter, Sunita. Her third daughter was born when Sunita was sixteen. Maya told us how proud and satisfied she was with each pregnancy, although each one meant nights without customers, a reduction of her income and a few debts. She is lucky to have a fixed client as well as her one-off customers, and she is sure that it was her fixed client who fathered her second and third daughters. He helped her to support herself and her daughters during the pregnancies.

Her eldest daughter, Anita, was just sixteen when she had her first sexual experience. This was with a man who had promised to marry her. After waiting for one year, she lost hope and started taking in commercial clients. She said she did this to take revenge on that man and on her mother. Maya was deeply upset when Anita joined the profession. Later, Sunita also joined the trade. Their mother was now too old to practise, and so helped her daughters out with child-care and domestic work. When her third daughter was six, she discussed her future with Anita and Sunita. None of them wanted her to join the profession. Although not educated themselves, they eagerly accepted a client's suggestion that the youngest should be sent away to school. By the time she was eight she was sent to a boarding school. At first they used to visit her but would never bring her back home. After the third year the girl did not miss her family as much.

We asked Sunita why she had taken such a decision. She replied, 'I and my elder sister had to join this profession, following our mother. But for our sister we want everything to be different. We want her to grow up in a healthy environment and have all the opportunities that we have missed. We do not want her to enter a painful and degrading life like ours. We live because of her. Otherwise there is nothing to look forward to.'

CHOOSING PARENTING

For many sex-workers their children represent hopes, dreams, new beginnings. They also represent a way out, a link with mainstream society, and an old age free of charity. Contrary to common belief, most do not want their daughters to join the trade, but want them to experience a stable married life.

Sex-workers who lose their earning power as they become old depend financially upon their children and look to them for security. Both daughters and sons support their mothers in old age, providing them with shelter and security. In India it is only the family that provides for the old. Once a single woman retires from the sex-trade, she leads a precarious existence. As the income of an elderly sex-worker declines, other earning members of the family are vital for survival.

Meera is in her late forties. She has been in the same red-light area for the last twenty-two years. She has left three times with different men but each time the relationship has broken down and she has had to return. She has a daughter from her first marriage. 'I have always wanted to live like a housewife but my circumstances have betrayed me.' Her daughter is a very bright and gentle girl. She studied up to Class 9 but left because of the taunts of students and staff. Now she is at a hostel and is completing her education. She wants to help her mother by earning her living. Her mother currently depends on a babu who has a family and who visits her regularly and gives around Rs.300 a month. She lives in one small room which has no electricity or running water. Her expectations of her daughter are very high and she waits for the day when her daughter will help her move out.

FLEXIBLE FAMILY NORMS

Like Meera's daughter, children of sex-workers may have been born out of previous marriages that broke down or out of previous relationships, current relationships or been fathered by clients. The absent, transitory or unknown figure of the father is usually not significant in the lives of the children. Many children are even sent away from the red-light area to live in hostels or with relatives, so the concepts of family and home are very transient and flexible. In practical terms sex-workers manage their parenting in a variety of ways; frequently without the support of their babus who rarely offer financial security or help out with actual parenting or domestic work.

Although mothers and daughters in India are traditionally restricted from living together once the daughter is married, women in the sex trade are free of such norms. Many daughters come back after marriage to live with their mothers and they help each other out financially. Because many women are the main breadwinners, managing households on their own and providing financial support to their families, traditional gender divisions such as who controls household budgets and household decision-making, and who does the household work are not rigidly imposed. In one large red-light area of Calcutta some men even do the cooking and household chores because the high number of clients leaves the women with absolutely no time for cooking. Ironically, despite a certain amount of freedom and relaxed restrictions on women that comes with being associated with the sex trade, many sex-workers and their daughters do aspire to live in a more traditional family setup, which is usually denied to them. Dowries are paid to get daughters married off. Mothers still aspire for their daughters to be secure in traditional marriages, even though in their own lives they have often experienced the hypocrisy and vulnerability of the marriage system. These middle-class aspirations too collapse when babus refuse to marry them, when children have to be sent away, when old age sees their men disappearing along with their looks and their money. What is left is the need to find a new livelihood, and a dependency on their children whose own opportunities in life have been restricted.

INFLUENCES OF THE ENVIRONMENT

Mothers who raise their children in the red-light areas do so without access to proper child-care, space or amenities, and have to watch their children grow up in unhygienic and unsafe surroundings. Children raised in red-light areas are vulnerable to sexual abuse, especially the girls. For no faults of their own, the children are stigmatized because of their mother's profession, frequently denied schooling and disowned by relatives. Because of the lack of child-care for single working mothers, many children roam the streets unattended. They often get sick from the dirt and are vulnerable to accidents. We have seen young children lying in the streets with pigs, or playing happily in areas dirty with animal and human excreta. One of the red-light areas has a dirty canal running right through it, which floods in the monsoon season and is surrounded by garbage and filth. Traffic is another hazard, though one that is shared with all urban children. We know of a child who was run over on the street. His legs were broken and not properly set. He now needs an operation to re-set them but his mother is afraid to send him to the hospital.

Rakesh is a little boy of four. Attached to his mother, he would run in and out of her room while she entertained clients. Once he ran in and refused to leave even though a client was present, who picked him up and hurled him out. The boy damaged his spinal chord and has not been able to walk since.

Recently, some attention has been turned on children in red-light areas because of their perceived vulnerability to HIV/AIDS. According to existing UNICEF/WHO studies, children in the red-light areas are the most vulnerable to the threat of HIV/AIDS. There have been predictions that by the end of the decade, if current trends continue, the rate of infection among Asians will exceed the present rate among Africans. (WHO has estimated that by the end of the decade, 10 million children will be on their own in Africa; orphaned or abandoned due to AIDS.) Children born to an HIV-infected mother have a one in three chance of being born with the virus, and then an 80-percent chance of dying by the age of five (UNICEF 1994).

Young girls raised in the red-light areas are particularly vulnerable to sexual abuse around the age of puberty, and it is at this time that mothers think of sending them elsewhere, often by marrying them off at an early age. Because of the atmosphere in which the daughters grow up, they often learn to relate to others, gain approval and attention, by using their own sexuality, which increases their vulnerability to sexual exploitation. Knowing this, mothers often make the difficult decision to send their daughters away. Even then, the child's development may have been affected by the influences of the environment, particularly on how she responds to sex. We met a ten-year-old girl whose mother is a sex-worker. She was sent to a residential home at an early age, but still remembers what she saw when she was with her mother. Like many children, she masturbates, but she touches herself quite openly. She told a counsellor that she used to peep under her mother's door and watch her do this for clients, and she learnt to copy her. A thirteen-year-old girl has told us how one of her mother's clients tried to rape her.

STIGMATIZING THE CHILDREN

Parveen was admitted into school and her mother kept her identity a secret. She went to school until she was in Class 9, but one day her identity was disclosed and she started being humiliated. When other students laughed at her she could bear it, but when one day a teacher looked at her and spat on the floor, she decided to leave the school.

It is not uncommon for children of sex-workers to be refused admission to schools. When they are admitted, they frequently drop out because they are ill-treated and taunted by other students. Munni, a Nepalese girl of eight, told us how she felt about growing up at home: 'I hate this place. I am never sent to school. I used to go to a school in this neighbourhood but soon they sent me away because I belong to this area. They called me a prostitute—I cried and cried and I did not go back. I hate all the men who come here. They squeeze me.'

A single-parent family in itself creates certain problems. Opening a bank account, applying for a ration card, seeking admission to school—all require a father's name. Just going to a government hospital means filling in a form with the father's name. The mother will often just lie or put in her present partner's name, but this could cause complications later on. Fortunately the term 'guardian' is slowly being introduced to replace 'father' in some areas, to stop this discrimination against single-parent families. In 1988 the West Bengal

Board of Secondary Education sent a notice to all schools ordering that the admission form be changed from 'father's name' to 'name of father/mother/guardian'. Schools by law cannot deny a child admission because she or he is unable to provide the name of the father. (This law was passed after Delhi sex-workers challenged the Supreme Court in 1992.) Government schools should in theory treat all applicants equally. In practice, however, children from the red-light areas are discriminated against in admission and forced to lie and conceal their identity. Other practical difficulties arise because of the different lifestyles of the children. For example, their mothers work late into the night, are unable to provide space and quiet for them to do their homework, or peace for them to go to bed in time. Most of the mothers are non-literate or neo-literate (80% according to the All Bengal Women's Union Study, 84% according to the AIIH&PH study), and so have their own limitations in supporting and understanding the demands of their children's schooling.

LIMITED OPPORTUNITIES

Very few daughters of sex-workers actually join the trade. As mentioned earlier, in the Sanlaap survey, only 6 out of 201 sex-workers who stated a reason for joining the profession, said that their mothers were sex-workers. Those who do join the sex trade usually do not go straight into the profession but return later on in their lives, perhaps after a failed marriage or when in need of money to support their families. For example, a mother told us that her daughter was always quite wayward, even though she was bright and went to school. She failed a couple of times in school and dropped out, then started having affairs with men at the age of thirteen, being used for sex in return for small presents. At fifteen she ran away with a boy from another neighbourhood. Her mother thought they might as well be married, but she was not even allowed entry into her lover's *bhadralok* or respectable, middle-class family. She soon became pregnant, and her lover left her. She is back in the red-light area, managing to make a living selling liquor. She is very bright and street-wise, and does not want to join the trade. Her relationship with her mother has deteriorated greatly. Her mother now encourages her to join the sex-trade. Her present business is insecure as she has no license to sell alcohol and could be closed down at any time.

Some sons get involved in the sex-trade, either directly as pimps or as trafficking agents, or more indirectly through working for political parties, through local clubs, selling drugs or alcohol. Youths in red-light areas are usually short on the qualifications and contacts necessary for securing formal sector jobs. Many go on to do manual work, for example, as mechanics in garages, in small industries, or running tea-shops in the local area. Unemployment and underemployment are very grave, however, and many have nothing much to do except hang around and do odd jobs when these are available.

COMMUNITY CHILD-CARE

One of the problems faced by mothers and children in red-light areas is the lack of appropriate child-care facilities. Informal systems do exist and have many positive aspects. Because of the absence of the joint family in the red-light areas, the traditional support-system of family elders is not available for sex-workers. Many mothers, such as Seema, simply leave their children outside during their working hours. Seema was a refugee from Bangladesh in the seventies. She began working as a housemaid but could not manage on the income. She met agents who introduced her to this profession. She now has four children and a fixed babu who comes once a week and pays her around Rs.300 a month. This amount covers her rent and she supplements her income by working independently as a sex-worker. One of her daughters has been admitted to a residential home while her other daughter and two sons live with her in one room. In the evenings when she entertains clients, her children stay outside in front of the temple nearby, or sometimes on the verandahs of neighbouring houses. She says she finds it humiliating and emphasizes that she is after all working for her children.

Because of the lack of extended family members to care for children, and the absence of formal child-care arrangements, a role has evolved for elderly sex-workers who work as child-minders for neighbours. This is also an important economic role for elderly women who themselves may be without family support. The child-minders are women like Parvati who is eighty-four years old. Deserted by her husband over thirty years ago, she moved to a red-light area and began caring for young children and babies of sex-workers. The mothers would breastfeed them from time to time in between servicing clients, while Parvati sat with them throughout the day. She told us that when the children were around five years of age, they would begin to pick up the ways of the street. They would start smoking at a very young age and would sip alcohol from the clients' glasses. ' The children are the closest emotional bond for the mothers, but what else can they do but close the door on a crying child when work has to be done?' She finds her work satisfying, and is paid enough to meet her basic needs.

Kakoli is a working mother who employs a neighbour to look after her child. She has a fixed babu, and earns about Rs.100 per day. She pays Rs.25 a day to a woman who looks after her daughter in the neighbourhood and who returns the child to her at night when she has finished working. Kakoli is unable to keep her daughter with her because she lives and works in one room. 'This way at least I can see her regularly. When she is older I will send her to live with her grandmother. By that time I will also be supporting my parents as my brothers are not taking care of them.' Kakoli is twenty-two years old.

At present sex-workers strive to make the best of what is available, leaving their children in the care of neighbours, relatives, former sex-workers or on the street while they work. As mentioned earlier, some women even go to other red-light areas to practise, renting shared rooms there on a daily basis, because they do not want to practise in the room with their children present. Formal child-care arrangements are scarce: even though more NGOs are opening creches in red-light areas, they do not always serve their purpose. They are not necessarily open during the late hours when the women are working, and so mothers have to organize their own child-care.

AWAY FROM HOME

Because of the problems of raising children in the red-light areas, many mothers choose to send their children away. They are then usually cared for by relatives who may even be un-aware of their mothers' profession. In these cases the mothers have to hide their profession from their children, and can only see them on visits. Others are sent to residential schools or hostels if their mothers can afford it, or if they are given fund-ing or a free placement through a charitable organization.

The 1988 study by the All Bengal Women's Union among Calcutta sex-workers found that over 40 percent of the chil-dren did not live with their mothers, but were with guardians, in hostels, and some had not even come to the red-light area when the mother joined the trade. This still means that ap-proximately 60 percent of the children were growing up in the red-light areas. Table 6.1 shows the different types and dis-tribution of child-care:

TABLE 6.1 Types of Child-Care

Neighbour is paid to look after the child	10
Child lives with guardians in home village	27
Child lives in school hostel	6
Child (born during marriage) lives with husband's family	4
Lives in same premises as mother (eg on a verandah or with a servant)	42
Total	89
(Of the 160 sex-workers interviewed, 71 had no children)	

Source: All Bengal Women's Union, 1988

The survey by Development Dialogue had slightly different findings: they found that just over 10 percent of the children were not living with their mothers. Out of 100 women sur-veyed in Bowbazar, Sett Bagan and Ram Bagan red-light ar-eas, 93 of a total of 104 children stayed with their mothers, only 8 were in the home village with relatives, 2 were in resi-dential homes or hostels, and 1 was working away. The moth-ers each sent between Rs.20-100 per month home for their children's upkeep if they were in their village (*Samya Shakti*, 5 and 6: 241).

Legally, under the Juvenile Justice Act a child can be removed from a mother who works in the sex industry or from a brothel. The policy of the government and also of many NGOs has been to protect the children by taking them elsewhere, usually into residential care. While the logic behind this approach is clear, institutional care does separate families; the homes are often located too far away for visits to take place, and the mothers' visits are often not encouraged because of the assumption that they are a bad influence on their children and are unfit to be parents simply because of their profession. This separation is difficult for both the children and the mothers.

SUPPORTING WORKING MOTHERS

Professional organizations working with children, such as UNICEF, and government schemes such as the Integrated Child Development Scheme (ICDS)[1] are notable by their absence in the red-light areas. Children of sex-workers have not been identified as a category with specific needs and problems, and there is an urgent need for information about appropriate ways of working with these children. Many NGOs that are working with the children need far more information and specialist help. More facilities in the red-light areas themselves would enable the children to remain with their mothers while offering them protection and an exposure to alternative lifestyles. Night-shelters in the red-light areas would be an excellent alternative if only there was more space for accommodation. The existing system of using elderly women as paid child-minders could be strengthened, and child-care facilities set up by outsiders should definitely employ local, elderly women. By not doing so, these interventions could threaten the livelihoods of the existing child-minders.

The way out in the long run is not to create more homes where children are taken away from their mothers and siblings, but to create other options within the area itself, and to fight for their acceptance into local schools to enable them to live with self-respect and dignity. Some activists are calling for reservations for children of sex-workers in the hope that even though the first generation will probably be stigmatized future generations will be free from the prejudice.[2] They believe that reservations could enable a generation of children to be educated and employed so that they could stand on their own feet and fight the stigmatization by being successful role models.

At present, however, children in the red-light areas must live with the ugly reality that they are considered to be different from other children, that society is not ready to accept them. On the contrary, they are rejected because of the environment they live in. We have to remember that a red-light area is not just a place where men go to buy sex. It is a place where all generations live, where children study, play, grow up. If we are serious about wanting to help these children we must advocate a fundamental shift in society's attitude to prostitution, and not just greater provision of protective homes where the children can only be temporarily sheltered.

NOTES

1. This is a large UNICEF-funded pre-school programme implemented by the Government of India. Local women teach pre-school children, who receive health check-ups and free meals.
2. A policy similar to affirmative action where such children would get preferential treatment for admission to schools, colleges and in the selection for jobs.

CHAPTER 7

Clients and Babus

Without the clients, there would be no sex industry; in other words, it is the demand from the male clients that causes the sex industry to come into existence. Understanding the needs of the clients is crucial to our discussion, as is an understanding of the range of client–sex-worker relationships. What happens to the relationship when the client becomes a regular customer? What do sex-workers expect and hope for in their relationships with regular customers? Because Sanlaap's work is with the women in the sex trade, we draw on the knowledge gained through informal interactions with them, as well as from the only known surveys of clients in West Bengal: surveys conducted in 1993 by AIIH&PH of clients and babus (Singh 1995), and a survey of truck drivers conducted by the Society for Research on Haemotology and Blood Transfusion, 1993. The AIIH&PH survey was conducted in the Sonagachhi red-light area, the only red-light area in Calcutta to cater to high- as well as low-income clients.

MALE SEXUAL NEEDS

A universal explanation for the existence of a sex industry is the uncontrollable sex drive of men. The availability of commercial sex is said to provide men with an outlet that allows them to continue a normal healthy life. A second assumption is that men are able to experiment with taboo or deviant sexual preferences that they are unable to express with their wives. This would mean that there is a high demand for sex other than straight sex with commercial sex-workers. Both arguments imply that other women are somehow protected by the existence of the sex trade.

In the course of our work we have found, however, that the needs of clients are more complex than simply unemotional sexual release. Men who do visit for quick sex may be visiting out of curiosity for their first sexual experience or as part of a night out with a group of friends. Visits are usually planned beforehand or are part of a routine. Businessmen use sex-workers in a very calculated way by providing women for sexual entertainment as part of a business deal. Among male migrants who live in all-male hostel accommodation, there is a custom of visiting sex-workers, not just because men want to experience the pleasure of sex but because they have other emotional needs that the sex-workers are able to fulfil.

Men are also influenced by social factors such as having economic power over women, being bombarded with media-images of women's bodies as commodities, and being part of a social system that condones men buying sex. The attraction is not only sexual. Marriages in India are not usually based on romantic love, but on fulfilling mutual needs, security and carrying out obligations to the husband's family. Romantic love, however, is idealized in popular culture. Relationships between men and women as portrayed in popular culture are freer than in most people's lives. While such relationships cannot be a reality for most women, men have the opportunity to seek out these experiences outside marriage, with mistresses and sex-workers. Many clients who visit sex-workers form relationships with them, usually without long-term commitment but with shared lifestyles beyond simply sex: social, as well as emotional and sexual factors, appear to be strong influences. Many of the clients do not come to the red-light areas for anonymous sexual release with a new woman each time, but regularly return to the same woman. Some develop an emotional attachment to the women they see, and others end up living with them, whether or not they are already married or have other relationships.

THE KIND OF CLIENT

The clients we discuss here are poor, lower middle and middle class men. They are primarily unskilled or semi-skilled workers, for example, rickshaw-pullers, traders, small shopkeepers, manual labourers, factory workers or those employed in small industries. Clients are also policemen, local anti-socials or hoodlums. If men can afford to visit women elsewhere, they do not go to red-light areas because of the unhygienic conditions. Wealthier men will pick up a woman and take her somewhere else, visit a floating sex-worker who does not work in a red-light area, or arrange for a higher-class call girl through a pimp or a known pick-up place such as a bar or a hotel.

Some small red-light areas cater to clients of a specific income bracket, whereas larger areas can cater to a more diverse range. Loker Math, for example, has only twenty-one houses where about fifty-five or sixty women work. All customers are from very low-income groups and can rarely pay more than Rs.25 a visit. Sonagachhi is the only red-light area that caters to high-income clients. AIIH&PH found that 45.5 percent of clients had an income of less than Rs.1,000 per month, while 13.6 percent had a monthly income of over Rs.2,500. The main occupation of the clients was described as business, while service was the second most common employment ('service' is generally used to describe government jobs). Students formed 8 percent of the clients. Among the clients, 87 percent were literate and 25 percent had been through higher education. The babus or the clients with whom the women had special arrangements, were found to be slightly less educated, with 74.3 percent literacy, only 9.1 percent of whom had been through higher education.

TEMPORARY CLIENTS

Clients who come for quick sex and are not known in the area are often travellers or men who are simply there out of curiosity. Some men do not develop a habit of regularly visiting commercial sex-workers and so will not be seen again after a few visits. Many of these clients are young men, adolescents, who are curious about sex and who do not bother to return after a few months once they have gained some experience and their curiosity has been satisfied. Many of the wealthier and educated young men who come for their first sexual experiences are introduced by their drivers. Taxi drivers and rickshaw-pullers also introduce new clients to an area. For these one-off clients the attraction is clearly non-emotional. Truck drivers who are regularly on the move visit sex-workers on the highways in different places. A survey of truck drivers in Uluberia, West Bengal, found that 94 percent of them visited commercial sex-workers, commonly from three to eight visits a month. The survey found that none of them told their wives about their visits. Most of the clients surveyed by AIIH&PH said that they visit sex-workers once or twice a week.

FIXED CLIENTS AND BABUS

Many of the clients regularly visit the same woman, for a period of a few months or for years. The longer the relationship, the more it becomes like a husband-wife relationship. Some of the regular clients pay fixed monthly sums, and some even live with their mistresses. A study of twenty-seven sex-workers in the Sett Bagan red-light area found that 60 percent of the women had been in a relationship with the same babu for periods ranging from six to twenty years. Half of the babus were married, and the wives sometimes knew about the mistresses who were seen as second wives. The wives, however, did not know that the women were sex-workers (Evans 1995).

Some of the regular clients are very organized about their visits. They will fix a set time every week or every month, and pay a fixed monthly amount. They might leave their own clothes in the women's rooms, stay overnight, the women will cook their favourite food for them, and they will have a friendship that is pleasant for both, although they are not necessarily emotionally close. Fixed clients pay less per visit than temporary ones, as the women are more financially secure with regular fixed clients. They will also give little extras when asked, such as tips during puja or other festivals that the more anonymous clients will not be obliged to give.

Some customers who visit the same women regularly do get emotionally involved and build up close friendships or relationships with them. Even though they might have families of their own, they become attached to a particular woman, often for several years, before leaving or moving to another. They will probably pay the woman a fixed monthly sum, as well as give presents, money for clothes or even a trip to a holiday resort or some other treat. The emotional attachment may or may not be reciprocated, and related issues such as his claims on her (whether or not he likes her to entertain other clients), and how the financial side of the relationship evolves, are details that individual couples work out.

Those who want oral, anal or other non-straight sex from sex-workers are more likely to return to the same woman because the whole transaction is simpler if the customer's preferences are already known and agreed upon. Some women refuse to perform certain kinds of sex and so negotiating the deal is more complicated and time-consuming with a new woman each time. Some men prefer visiting the same woman regularly simply because it saves time having to chit-chat and make small talk before sex. In other words, visiting the same woman regularly can be just a more efficient way of arranging the visits.

FIXED CLIENTS AND PARENTING

The fixed clients have varying levels of commitment to the women they visit. If the woman becomes pregnant, most clients stop visiting, although sometimes if a man thinks that the child is his, he becomes even more involved in the woman's life. We have known of several fixed clients who stop their visits temporarily during the pregnancy but still send money, resuming their visits again after the birth.

We have been surprised at how many fixed clients do want to be involved in the lives of the children whom they believe they have fathered. We know one woman who sent her child to live with her relatives in a village. Her babu sends money to the village regularly for the child's upkeep, even though he never sees the child. In another area, a fixed client took his child away from the mother as soon as she was born and gave her to a friend of his to raise, not telling anyone that the child was his. The mother never sees her child and yet agrees that what her babu did was for the best. They both think that the red-light area is not a suitable place to raise children.

Gita has a regular client who has his own family living in a nearby lane. He never spends the night with her, although he gives her a regular amount of money for her maintenance. She has a child, whom they both believe is his. He helps to support the child and looks after her. His family knows about the situation and has had to accept it. He wants her to stop taking other clients, and they fight about this regularly, but she refuses to do so as she needs the extra money.

MISMATCHED EXPECTATIONS

Fixed clients are an attractive proposition to most sex-workers because they can offer relative financial security, decreasing dependence on the unpredictable trade of one-off, temporary clients. Sex-workers also value the prospect of a stable love relationship, and gain in respectability by reducing the number of their clients to one or two fixed men. Many sex-workers hope that they will be able to leave the profession and lead a respectable life as a wife in a traditional relationship, although few babus are able to offer this to them because of their own lack of interest, their inability to support a wife financially, or pressures from their own families. The expectations of the two parties in these fixed relationships therefore usually do not match. Family pressures on fixed clients often prevent them from marrying their mistresses.

Take Maya, for example. She had some income from renting rooms in a red-light area and so took in just a couple of men as clients. Both became her fixed clients, and both fell in love with her. The first was a shopkeeper, a paying client, who always said he would marry her, but eventually succumbed to pressures to marry someone chosen by his family. Maya continued seeing the second client and succeeded in annoying the first. She became pregnant by the first man, and he wanted her to be faithful to him even though he was married. She said she would only be faithful to him if he took her away from the red-light area and gave her the respectability of being in a 'proper' relationship. Now the two men are fighting over her. We asked of her, wasn't she scared that they might harm her? She replied that as long as she remained in her own neighbourhood she had nothing to be scared of; she had more hoodlums she could rely on than they did. They were the outsiders. But she still wants to leave her neighbourhood if she could be in a respectable relationship with either of the men.

Urmila would not accept a situation where she was simply being kept by one man in a red-light area. She had a regular client who fell in love with her and said he would marry her. She left the red-light area with him and the two were married, but they soon found out that his family would not accept her, and she could not live with him. He did not confront his family; suggesting instead that Urmila return to the red-light area where he would maintain her and visit her whenever he could. She felt hurt that he could so easily send her back to the red-light area and decided that she did not want to be a 're-spectable prostitute'. If she could not be his real wife, living with him in a respectable area, she might as well carry on as before and entertain other clients. The couple came to blows and her husband lost his temper and injured her with a knife. He returned another time with his family and some other men and threatened her. She fled to the police who padlocked her room for a month while she stayed elsewhere, after which time she returned and began working again. She has now resolved the situation with her 'husband' who continues to visit and—despite their being legally married—has been relegated to the status of being just one of her several fixed clients.

SEX-WORKERS' PREFERENCES

Many younger women prefer the known half-hour clients who do not want to be emotionally involved, but who visit the same woman each time. They can charge more to the half-hour clients, and remain independent and free to entertain other customers. It may be sexually safer to see known men as it cuts down the number of sexual partners with whom a woman comes into direct contact. The women are also safer from violence if the clients are known to them as their behaviour is also known and predictable. A new customer, on the other hand, may demand sexual variations disliked by the women; they may be unpleasant or refuse to pay.

Older women who are more financially insecure begin to

appreciate the fixed clients who can give them a regular monthly sum and who might also be able to offer a satisfying relationship. Even though these clients tend to leave after a few years, during the period of their steady visits, they do offer stability. For the younger women this is a disadvantage as it is harder to build up new clients once they have become associated with particular men and are seen to 'belong' to certain customers. We feel that the younger sex-workers—those in their twenties—are more clinical and detached from their work and so prefer their clients to be similarly detached. Most women do not like clients to stay the night, especially if they have children living with them.

All women fear the local hoodlums as clients. The latter's influence in the community means that women receive little support from others if things turn ugly. Some of the hoodlums are also landlords and are inclined to be violent and claim young good-looking women for themselves, often without the women's consent. Hoodlums from other areas also come as customers. The women who are in the chukri system, and who are almost in bondage to pimps, have no control over the selection of clients and are not able to form relationships of their choosing until they leave that system and begin working independently. As expected, many clients are unconcerned about the women whose bodies they use, but there have been several cases where clients have been helpful. For example, recently a local newspaper carried a report of a 'kind-hearted client' who helped two bonded teenagers to escape from a Bombay brothel and return to their homes in West Bengal (*The Telegraph*, 20 Nov 1995). Sonagachhi police are often informed about new minors working in the area by clients who are concerned about their welfare. The vicious treatment meted out to sex-workers is usually by clients who are already known as anti-socials.

SEXUAL BEHAVIOUR

A study by AIIH&PH in 1992 found that straight sex (penovaginal) is universal among commercial sex-workers of whom 74 percent said they also engaged in oral sex, although this figure dropped to 38.1 percent in an evaluation study by the same organization in 1993. Group sex was practised by 27.3

percent in 1992, although again a variation occurred in the 1993 evaluation study which found that 48.7 percent admitted to having done so. While these disparities may be explained by changes in sexual behaviour as a result of the intervention project, they may also reveal that statistics on sensitive sexual behaviours are difficult to collect and not necessarily a reliable indicator. For example, different findings were mentioned in one in-depth qualitative study in Sett Bagan where most sex-workers reported that the demand for oral sex was increasing (Evans 1995). All the surveys do reveal that customers engage in sexual behaviours with sex-workers that are still taboo within marriage. Evans reports that oral, anal and vaginal sex are demanded by clients, as well as masturbation and the indulgence of men's fantasies. This information seems to support the argument that some men visit sex-workers for activities that are unacceptable within marriage, although the most common sexual behaviour between sex-workers and their clients is still straight peno-vaginal sex.

POWER AND CONTROL

Relationships with fixed clients vary in terms of power and control. Couples in long-term relationships generally take on the same roles and obligations of man and wife. Most long-term babus expect to exercise control over the movements of their mistresses, and this traditional aspect of the relationship is accepted by many of the women. Soma, for example, has a fixed client who gives her a regular income and, although she has other customers, she depends heavily on his goodwill. She started taking karate classes and her babu had no objections. After a while she also started attending drama workshops that Sanlaap was organizing in order to present a play for International Women's Day. Her babu did not like the idea of her acting in the play. When he realized that she would be performing in public, he told her that she had to stop. Even though she had been enjoying the workshops and was looking forward to the performance, she agreed to do so. At the end of the day she could not afford to displease him. Even the fixed clients who pay for their relationships cannot help but be patriarchal.

Some of the babus take advantage of the women's earnings. Those who are supported by the sex-workers may become less concerned about earning for themselves, and may begin to push their mistresses to work harder and earn more money. This is despite the babus not doing their share of the workload of household chores or raising children in return. Babus are actually referred to by sex-workers as those who 'give-money' and those who 'eat money' (Evans 1995). Interestingly, when discussing legal issues with sex-workers we have pointed out that living off a sex-worker's earnings is illegal. Sex-workers disagree and feel that this clause is morally wrong as they should have the right to support their babus, just as a husband should have the right to support his wife.

For most sex-workers, a life of respectability outside the sex trade is only possible with marriage. The status of being a traditional housewife is seen as a compensation for the loss of independence. Renu was practising as an independent sex-worker without a mashi or a pimp. When she married her fixed client she stopped seeing other customers. Her husband is a driver and so earns enough to support them both, and his family are in Bihar and do not have much influence over him. She now describes herself as a housewife. She says she is lucky to have found a man who loves her so much. Even though she had been working independently and supporting herself earlier, she was very happy to give it up for a 'respectable' life. They live in the room were she practised as a sex-worker because it is cheap and they are accepted in the area. Elsewhere she would have to keep her previous life a secret.

CLIENTS OUTSIDE RED-LIGHT AREAS

We know little about the clients who visit the floating sex-workers because Sanlaap's work does not involve trying to access them. We have only been able to talk to a few women who live in a red-light area but work outside. Many of the rich clients who take these women out in their cars will either go to hotels, or else will just have sex with them in the car. Certain places where pimps and sex-workers operate are known to groups of clients who live, work or study together. Sunita, for example, lives in a red-light area but does not work there any more because she has children at home. She goes to a place in the centre of the city where by the banks of the Hooghly covered boats are on hire. Some of the boat owners act as pimps. Clients come to this place and they call over the women who stand nearby, waiting. Sunita is one of the women who will get into a boat with the boatman and the client and then have sex in the boat. We asked her about the type of clients who come here. The majority of them, she tells us, are young college students, and physically the work is easy. We asked her what she thought of them. 'Generally the customers are young and very excitable. Usually I just have to touch them, so the work is very easy.' On her side she is quite happy because it pays well and her children are not around to see what she does. For the students, the boats cater to their needs because the pimps have become known to them, the boats afford privacy and safety, and they don't have to visit the red-light areas which they would find dirty and overcrowded.

Other clients who do not need to visit the red-light areas are those who can afford to go to the notorious bars and hotels in the centre of Calcutta, or take women out in vehicles. Pimps operate in many hotels, and even arrange women for business-men who 'order' them for their business partners or clients. If they are holding a party for their business clients, they might buy the services of several women for the night. Many of these clients are regular in the sense that they will use the same pimp each time and so the same group of women will be used. Hotel clients are also rich locals and tourists. They pay around Rs.200–300 for an evening with a woman, and if she stays the night then anything up to Rs.1,500. The women who get these kind of clients only have to work occasionally, often one week a month, to make a lot of money. Some are kept by them as mistresses. But the average sex-worker will never get clients who pay as much because they do not have access to the network of middlemen who cater to the demands of wealthy men and organize the women for them.

In brief, clients are not a homogeneous group, nor is the distinction between clients and babus clear-cut. It appears that the demands of clients and the relationships between clients and sex-workers are very diverse. The existence of so many fixed clients reveals that both parties are often happier being with known people than with strangers. The sexual act is not always an anonymous business transaction. Socially, fixed clients offer a safer and more efficient way of working, and it may also be sexually safer for both as it cuts down on the number of partners.

Ironically, the more involved they get the more the men begin to behave 'like husbands'; and many of these women have already had bad experiences with husbands. As they grow older, however, the women need and value the emotional and financial stability of long-term relationships, and so emotionally invest more in their fixed clients. Most sex-workers are sure that their fixed clients fathered their children, rather than any of their other clients, which shows that having a known father, who it is hoped will take some responsibility, remains important. This is ironic as sex-workers' experiences with clients put them in a privileged position to understand the hypocrisy behind so many supposedly monogamous relationships. Yet, because of their own financial insecurities, they have no choice but to aspire to a similar relationship.

The sheer numbers of men visiting sex-workers every day means that clients cannot be considered abnormal. The whole point of the sex trade is to cater to the needs and desires of men. It is likely that the sex trade exists because patriarchal societies give undue emphasis to the male sexual urge and to gratifying men's desires. Definitely, while both men and women have emotional and sexual needs which are not being met within marriage, only men have the option of finding an outlet for self-gratification. And while the class of women who gratify these needs are branded as public women and are ostracized from society, the men are able to keep their visits or relationships secret from their families, find approval from other men, and continue to lead a publicly respectable life. Behind this hypocrisy, both men and women try to maximize their interests, spending money, earning money, bringing their different and unequal interests into each encounter and each relationship. It must be remembered that the sex trade, where survival and gratification meet in such diverse ways, has as its objective the gratification of the needs of men.

CHAPTER 8

Interventions and Initiatives

'Instead of trying to reform them [the sex-workers], we must reform social attitudes which treat social victims as criminals.'

— Madhu Kishwar, activist,
The Illustrated Weekly, 25 April 1992

WHENEVER WE INFORM people that Sanlaap works with sex-workers, the common response is to ask how easy it is to rehabilitate them. Many people assume that rehabilitation is the only possible intervention, and this is, in a sense, a hangover from the past when policies were either health-related or geared to bring the women out of prostitution. Rehabilitation of sex-workers is in fact notoriously difficult, for many reasons. Few people are willing to employ an ex-sex-worker. Most employment schemes offer only minimal earnings and are not attractive, financially or otherwise, to sex-workers. Most important, attempting to rehabilitate a handful of sex-workers cannot have an impact on the sex trade as a whole.

WHAT IS REHABILITATION?

In 1990, Savdhaan, a NGO, sent approximately 1,000 sex-workers from Bombay to their home states in South India. By 1992, more than 500 were known to have returned to the red-light area. It was reported at the time that many of these women had been forced to leave the profession against their will. Why was this done? Vinod Gupta of Savdhaan was quoted as saying, 'It is everybody's duty to make sure that prostitution does not exist' (*The Illustrated Weekly of India*, 25 April 1992). The act of rehabilitation was clearly his own agenda rather than that of the women themselves, which is why it did not work.

Many sex-workers do want new jobs, particularly the elderly women. Since sex-work is intrinsically a part of society, it is not possible to 'stop' it or to succeed with a 'welfarist' approach. The women do not need 'reforming', but they can benefit from the help of some outside interventions that are tailored specifically to their needs. The situation in the red-light areas is not static by any means. It is changing, partially as a result of targetted NGO and government interventions, as well as initiatives by sex-workers themselves. There are certainly several areas of activity where a more favourable climate is being created by and for the sex-workers.

In Calcutta, broadly speaking, sex-workers' own organizations such as Mahila Sangha, Nari Kalyan Samiti and Abahelita Mahila Samiti have sprung up around social action issues, and have later gone on to bring in outside support and services to the area. These groups have formed of their own initiative around a particular dispute or issue, and have later become entry points for NGOs and the government in their attempts to reach the population of the red-light areas with welfare or development programmes. The extent to which they have retained their focus on social action and have managed to evolve successfully as a group has varied.

The government provides a small number of welfare and health interventions, generally being a far less significant presence in the areas than NGOs other than through the AI-IHPH's STD/HIV Intervention Programme on health as well as social and legal issues. While NGOs aspire to a more empowerment-oriented approach, using the language of women's rights and often advocating broader social, economic and political changes, on the ground they are generally providing welfare programmes that substitute in the absence of the government, and replicate rather than challenge many weaknesses of mainstream approaches of service-provision. NGOs are constrained by their funding and have to develop on paper a strategy that appeals to donor agencies and to current trends such as community participation and challenging gender issues. As can be appreciated, it is far easier to learn the language of current issues in development than to implement them. Many NGOs in practice lack the skills, experience and access to training that would allow them to fulfil their promised agendas. At the same time the 'conference culture' ensures that visibility is guaranteed to the articulate and charismatic few who rarely admit to the difficulties faced by their organizations in implementation.

NGO INTERVENTIONS

We know of at least thirteen NGOs based in and around Calcutta who claim to be working directly with sex-workers. In addition there are others that are issue-based, for example, those organizations working on drug addiction that include sex-workers among their beneficiaries. There is just one NGO currently working with and prioritizing clients: the Bhoruka Research Centre that targets truck drivers.

Many truck drivers and their helpers, as their assistants are called, visit sex-workers who stand on the main highways and also visit red-light areas. The Bhoruka Public Welfare Trust is working with truck drivers in Howrah District at the Uluberia check-post. Truck drivers have to stop at the check-post between one hour to ten days to complete formalities with their registration papers. The check-post is therefore a place where many drivers and their helpers can be reached as they wait for their papers to be cleared. Bhoruka has set up a drop-in centre in the area, where trained social workers build rapport with the men and discuss STDs and HIV/AIDS with them. The centre also offers treatment facilities, information, testing for syphilis and hepatitis B, as well as voluntary HIV-testing and counselling. It also promotes condom-use. Some pioneering research has been done by Bhoruka on the attitudes and practices of the truck drivers who visit sex-workers: 94 percent of the truck drivers they have surveyed visit commercial sex-workers, but only 24 percent of them have ever used a condom.

Bhoruka is targetting a group of clients who engage in high-risk behaviour who can easily be reached and identified by their occupation.

Development Dialogue is a NGO that runs creches in the Sonagachhi and the Rambagan red-light areas. These are linked to a mid-way home in Murshidabad where the children can live after graduating from the creche. They are also planning to involve the mothers of these children in an income-generating project alongside the mid-way home so that they can be re-united with their children and ultimately begin an alternative life together away from the sex industry. Several women are currently undergoing skills-training for an income-generating activity. Development Dialogue also runs a separate papad or pappadom project in Murshidabad which, as discussed earlier, supplies many women to the sex industry. Development Dialogue is creating economic opportunities for women in this area so that fewer women are forced or tempted to migrate to become sex-workers. The overall objectives are therefore to prevent women from joining the industry, to provide wider opportunities to children of sex-workers, and to rehabilitate a specific group of practising or elderly sex-workers by offering them alternative employment.[1]

CINI (ASHA)[2] works with slum children in Sealdah, Bowbazar, Rambagan, Tollygunge and other areas. They come across many sexually exploited children, as well as children of sex-workers. They run evening drop-in centres for children, night shelters, and a short-stay home for vulnerable girls. Mothers' meetings are held regularly to discuss the progress of the children. Other problems faced by the women are raised and discussed but on the whole the intervention is explicitly child-focused. Girls from the home are admitted to boarding schools after a period of about one year in the home. During this time they receive counselling and are encouraged to learn to relate to other children. This is especially emphasized with the children from red-light areas because many face psychological problems; for example, because girls learn to use their sexuality to gain attention from adults and their peers, CINI (ASHA) encourages a period of readjustment to learn new ways of interacting with people away from commercial sex. Each girl's long-term association with CINI (ASHA) even after leaving the home is seen as a support that reduces her chances of becoming a sex-worker, even when she eventually return to her mother during holidays or after graduating from boarding school. The direct benefit to the mothers is primarily child-care support, and alleviating their worries about their children's futures—worries that are frequently cited as one of their major concerns.[3]

Cathedral Relief Service (CRS) is working in fourteen slums in Calcutta. One of them is the Bowbazar red-light area. Working through a local club, they started a small training project for teenage girls. CRS donated a sewing machine and a knitting machine on which the girls practise tailoring and knitting. They are also taught embroidery. The training process is still going on as they have only been in session for one year. CRS is supplying the materials free of charge. Later on, the products will be marketed through CRS's own outlets, and each item guarantees a fixed amount to the producer. While CRS talks of economic independence for the girls and hopes the project will provide an alternative to sex-work, they envisage that monthly earnings will not reach more than a maximum of Rs.400. Although a marketing bottleneck is cited as the reason, in actual fact the skills taught are only renumerative enough to provide a part-time, supplementary income.[4]

Jabala is a smaller organization than the other NGOs, and has been running classes for children in Bowbazar for just a year. It has run on voluntary contributions with the help of volunteers from outside and with a couple of local helpers and educators. Thirty to forty children from the red-light area, aged between five to thirteen, undergo 'behavioural therapy' through creative activities and physical exercises. They also go out on day trips, to cultural events and participate in functions and performances. Under pressure from the mothers, Jabala is introducing more school-related activities such as help with homework and tuition to supplement school-work. All the children attending Jabala's classes also attend government schools. Jabala feels that these children have to be strong enough to transcend the labels that stigmatize them, and always sees them as children in their own right and not as children of sex-workers. Jabala plans to concentrate on im-

proving and consolidating the work in the school rather than
on expanding their programmes, although they are also planning to do some work on HIV/AIDS in the future. The team of
volunteers works very informally and rather erratically with
the children. They have succeeded in creating a lot of interest
in drama and drawing, although the benefits of this are rather
intangible.[5]

The Centre for Contemporary Communication (CCC) focuses
on awareness-raising. CCC is a small NGO of four people currently working on a one year project that reaches out to high
school students (Classes 11 and 12) with information and education on HIV/AIDS. Approaching HIV/AIDS within a broad social
context, the work includes advocacy with school principals,
teachers and parents, awareness with students and also involves discussions with principals about how HIV/AIDS can be
integrated into the school curriculum as a whole. One focus
group discussion session with students covers the issue of
prostitution. Students are encouraged to talk about, for example, the status of sex-workers in India, the need for the sex
trade and the isolation or integration of sex-workers into mainstream society.[6]

When CCC initially approached 147 high schools in Calcutta,
twenty-six agreed to discuss a collaboration. Finally CCC became associated with just eight schools. Most schools were
reluctant to participate because of a lack of interest in
HIV/AIDS. The schools believe that students are not sexually
active and therefore not at risk and they wished to avoid con-
troversy. The sexual behaviour of adolescents is still a strong
taboo subject. What emerges again is that the HIV/AIDS epidemic opens up the issue of sexuality and commercial sex for
discussion, which could lead to more awareness in mainstream
society about the status of sex-workers. CCC has faced problems in carrying out awareness-raising activities. Its attempt
to bring the sex-workers face to face with students on World
AIDS Day 1995 was opposed by the Government of West Bengal, its funding agency, through the State AIDS Cell that falls
within the Ministry of Health and Family Welfare. Its programme of events included exhibitions, activities and discussions and was primarily for students. One event was a meeting
between the Jadavpur University's School of Women's Studies

and sex-workers, which went off well. Another event was a proposed meeting of high school students of Classes 11 and 12 with sex-worker representatives of Mahila Samanyaya women's committees that was cancelled as the government objected to the sex-workers meeting students even though the school principals had agreed to it.

This incident is a sad reflection on the government; while they are willingly going ahead with projects that treat sex-workers as passive beneficiaries of health programmes, they are unwilling to confront the larger social issues surrounding the problem of prostitution. By denying the sex-workers a platform in mainstream society, they are also holding back an important opportunity for a more effective fight against HIV/AIDS.

Sanlaap has a very explicitly woman-focused approach to its work and describes itself as a women's rights centre. It is managed and staffed overwhelmingly by women. At the project level Sanlaap runs a home for daughters of sex-workers that is located on the outskirts of Calcutta. The fifteen residents attend local schools, engage in sports, arts and crafts, and study block-printing as a vocational skill. The home houses its own block-printing training unit and some of the girls are following this up by undergoing a formal diploma course at a government-run training institute.

Sanlaap has a presence in seven Calcutta red-light areas: Kalighat, Diamond Harbour, Amtala, Kidderpore, Sonagachhi, Sett Bagan and Bagerhat. In most of these areas Sanlaap is supporting local clubs or groups to run creches and educational classes for the local children. As the organization develops it is trying to build on this work to introduce a more challenging and forward-looking agenda. A particular focus is on cases of violence against women, using its links with the police to ensure proper registration and follow-up of cases. Sanlaap tries to build links with senior police members and women's cells in order to offer practical support to sex-workers who are victims of violence or who need to interact with the police for other reasons. The staff and sex-workers have been trained on legal issues, and Sanlaap plans to work more intensively on issues of trafficking and police harassment, as well as lobbying for sex-worker's rights at the state level.

GOVERNMENT INTERVENTIONS

The All-India Institute of Hygiene and Public Health (AIIHPH) is a central government institution and implements a HIV/STD intervention programme focusing on HIV/STD-awareness and prevention among sex-workers in almost all the city's red-light areas. A group of sex-workers in each area is trained to become peer educators who distribute condoms and teach other sex-workers about HIV. At the same time, free clinics are available to sex-workers, flying sex-workers and clients in the red-light areas. Sex-workers receive information about STDs and are encouraged to convince clients to use condoms. The incidence of STDs has fallen in the areas where AIIHPH is working, and HIV rates have remained low in Calcutta red-light areas as compared to many other Indian cities. As a fall-out of the programme, AIIHPH has become an important employer of sex-workers, offering alternative or supplementary work as peer educators to a large number of women. The AIIHPH programme, perhaps more than any other programme, has had a significant impact on the red-light areas. Although not initially espousing empowerment as a specific objective, the peer educators themselves have gained a lot in terms of exposure, confidence, financial security and education through their work with the Institute. For example, the peer educators are the most motivated students of literacy classes being run in red-light areas because they are very clear about their personal need for literacy. They realize it will help their work and their chances of doing well with AIIHPH. Other motivated learners are those women who want to become peer educators. Ironically, although the Institute is working towards very clear objectives, focusing on STDs/HIV, it has had the additional success of training sex-workers in alternative employment. None of the small income-generation projects run by well-meaning NGOs can match what AIIHPH has done for the sex-workers in terms of offering alternative and regular employment, enabling the sex-workers to develop what they feel is a more worthy social identity.

The project is now also dealing directly with wider social goals. Under the guidance of the project, a cooperative of sex-workers has been formed that plans to begin income-generation projects and market condoms at a subsidized rate. Women's groups in each red-light area known as Mahila Samanyaya Committees have been established and are taking up need-based social and legal issues. Most of the issues taken up by sex-workers now in Calcutta's red-light areas are centred around and emerging from these committees.[7] The convention of 1200 sex-workers from all over India that was held in Calcutta on 30 April 1996 was a result of the initiative of the Mahila Samanyaya Committees (see Chapter 3).

The AIIHPH programme has been funded partly by the British Overseas Development Administration (ODA) as part of a three-year £1.5 million STD prevention and treatment project. This project has also worked with a network of local NGOs, aiming to develop to a significant level their understanding and competence in the field of sexual health and related issues such as counselling, communication and project planning.

The Government of India itself has recently taken initiatives to target the red-light areas with welfare and social development projects. The Department of Women and Children, Government of India, has established an advisory cell and has instructed state governments to set up advisory bodies with representatives from NGOs, academic institutions, medical bodies, the National Commission on Women, and so on. A national-level consultation was held in Bombay at the end of 1994, and regional consultations took place going throughout 1995. This has been part of a consultation period to prepare for creating government schemes for the red-light areas. The type of projects that will emerge cannot be anticipated as the process of consultation is still continuing, but it is known that funds have been committed, and the government has made an official statement indicating its willingness to work with sex-workers.

In the meantime, the government is funding several projects—such as homes for children of sex-workers—through general welfare schemes organized by the Department of Social Welfare. The government has also expressed an interest in starting Integrated Child Development Scheme (ICDS) creches for pre-school children in the red-light areas and some applications are pending. Unfortunately, the general isolation of the red-light areas means that government programmes that reach other slums are rarely found in red-light areas. This is by default rather than by design as staff do not like to visit these areas and they are easily by-passed: a fact that suggests the need for special targetted programmes.

Although the state is bound by law under Section 21 of the Prevention of Immoral Traffic Act to establish and maintain protective homes for sex-workers, there are no such homes in West Bengal. As mentioned earlier, sex-workers going through the legal system are kept in remand homes which are ill-equipped to provide the care, protection or rehabilitation required. Girls rescued from trafficking are also sent to remand homes, although they have not committed a crime. Liluah Home is such a place where women awaiting trial are kept, built to house sixty-five women, it is always crowded with well over a hundred. Even basic accommodation is lacking—some women sleep under beds and on floors because of lack of space and furniture. At the time of our visit, only two out of the seven fans were working, and a TV that had been donated to the home was standing unused in disrepair. A shortage of water meant that the bathrooms were filthy. The drains were overflowing; the residents preferred to bathe in a pond in the courtyard that was unclean and was the cause of rampant skin infections. Homes like these resemble jails even though the residents are awaiting their court cases and have not even been sentenced. The supervisors even walk around with *lathis* or sticks.

The architecture at Liluah is such that different groups of inmates are kept in different buildings. The sex-workers are kept all together in one building that is the only one, apart from the one for violent criminals, which is kept under lock and key. The inmates are thus confined and inactive for most of the day and can only leave the building at scheduled times, for meals, for instance. The state of these homes has an impact on the sex trade as a whole because even the police know that the women prefer to give money to be released from the lock up, rather than be sent to such a place.

ANALYSIS OF INTERVENTIONS

We would like to make some general comments that could stimulate debate and lead to more awareness about gender-

gender sensitive issues

sensitive approaches to interventions in red-light areas. The criticisms reflect weaknesses and blind spots in all organizations, including our own.

Child Focused Projects

needs assessment of RLA

Many of the programmes just mentioned work with children and concentrate on their predictable welfare needs as do the majority of such programmes throughout the country. While their objectives are laudable, we feel they could be more need-based, that is, catering to the specific needs of the children, the working mothers and the communities. Training teachers who work with children in red-light areas would upgrade the interventions, as many projects use unskilled or inappropriately trained teachers. Special workshops could be held for teachers and supervisors, so that they have a better understanding of their work and their role. At present, most creches and classes in red-light areas are staffed by local women whose main qualification is literacy, or else by outsiders who may not fully understand the problems faced by the children. Child-to-child learning could be encouraged to stimulate the process and reduce dependence on outsiders.[8] More creative approaches to learning and production of learning materials dealing with specific problems faced by children of sex-workers would also help to make the programmes more effective.

Unemployment and lack of income is a problem for elderly sex-workers, and as we have seen, traditionally they are given paid work as child-minders. This provision could be maintained and strengthened if projects with children employed elderly ex-sex-workers as teachers and supervisors.

Many creches are not open at times when the children are most vulnerable on the streets. More often than not, child-care or education projects finish early whereas the mothers work late. This suits the needs of the staff rather than the beneficiaries. By not fixing timings around the mother's working hours, they can only partially meet the children's practical need for a secure and learning environment during the late hours. The possibility of extending the creches and classes into night shelters could be explored, and of extending the role of the teachers to that of counsellors.

Recognizing that sex-workers are both paid workers and mothers who need child-care during their working hours is also important in strategic terms, as it moves away from a focus on women as mothers to an acknowledgement of their other role as household earners. Although this seems obvious when working in the red-light areas, it continues to be overlooked by some of the more welfare-oriented projects that still focus on women solely in their traditional role as mothers. Interventions with children can play an important role in alleviating the burden of child-care, therefore allowing women more time to do paid work. Interventions that want to focus on economic issues could see child-care in this light, rather than simply focusing on the obvious income-generation projects.

Some projects working with children adhere to a general cultural ideal that marriage and family offers future security for girls, and do not prepare the girls to be financially independent. These interventions are considered complete once the girls are safely married off; yet their troubles simply do not end with marriage. Women remain vulnerable if they live lives of dependency within marriage. Girls should still be equipped with skills that would allow them to earn an independent living if the marriage ends in separation, widowhood, or if they need to contribute to the family income even after marriage. The type of education and ideology promoted in child-care projects and homes is crucial to the success of the project if it aims to provide the children with realistic opportunities for the future. Failing to equip girls with skills for the future while sending boys on apprenticeships is a sexual stereotyping that further discriminates against girls.

Health Projects

A problem with many projects, for example, those that only focus on STDs/HIV, is that they again see the women only in one role, this time as commercial sex-workers and not as women in relationships, mothers, heads of households and so on. Sex-workers have sex with a variety of men, from long-term partners to one-off, temporary clients. By perceiving sex-workers only in their professional role we ignore their behaviour outside their work, and omit the issue of safe sex with babus. Advocating condom-use only with clients is hardly effective if the women do not use them with their babus.

Health projects can often meet women's own needs more effectively by working in a more holistic way, for example, dealing with their non-sexual health problems as well as sexual health problems that are lesser known but equally important to sex-workers. Working through doctors or medical personnel who are trained in communication skills and who are sensitive to women's social and psychological needs, apart from simply their medical health needs, could increase the effectiveness of these programmes. This is particularly so when doctors are expected to train and educate sex-workers. It should be realized that medical knowledge alone is not enough; communication skills and participatory learning methods could be a part of the doctor's training.

It has to be stressed that broader social issues are central to the women's ability to control their health. Education about STDs and condom-use, even with free distribution of condoms, is simply not enough. Projects that empower women to increase their bargaining power—both financially and socially—are crucial to the long-term success of health programmes. For example, promoting group formation and strengthening existing groups is a crucial intervention in the long term if sex-workers are to be able to demand that clients use condoms.

Income-Generation Projects

Income-generation projects that train young girls in traditionally female skills are rarely well thought out or accompanied by any assessment of the market needs for the product concerned and of the earning potential of that skill. Some stereotypical income-generation projects such as embroidery for girls cannot be seen as providing alternative livelihood options. The idea behind these projects is, more often than not, to give the women a skill that will provide them with pin money—small amounts that will supplement a larger income that is assumed will be forthcoming from a husband. This assumption is particularly inappropriate in red-light areas where the failings of the traditional family system and the dangers for dependent women who are not able to earn an independent livelihood are so obvious.

In theory, employment and training projects for girls can be an important entry point to challenge more general employment restrictions on women. Women and girls of the red-light areas can be trained in skills that have a high earning potential and may even be non-traditional for women, giving them the chance to be economically independent while at the same time challenging the gender division of labour. Non-traditional skills such as carpentry, electronics or driving are more likely to offer a better income, as traditional skills for women have generally evolved within the stereotype of women's need only for pin-money and traditional women's work tends to be lower paid. Learning skills that can offer a decent livelihood are particularly important when working in red-light areas, where alternative employment schemes for sex-workers are notoriously difficult because of the challenge of providing work with an equivalent income.

Local Power Groups

The long-term goals of projects need to be clear because there is a tendency for these to get lost in the day-to-day management of an organization. All NGO interventions require cooperation with local people who have vested interests in the sex industry. Most of the Calcutta NGOs have to work through local youth clubs that are male dominated and heavily politicized. They are forced to operate within existing structures, depending heavily on the cooperation of those who participate in and benefit from the sex industry. This does act as a constraint for the NGOs and also restricts their autonomy as they can only work within the boundaries approved of and sanctioned by the local power groups. The clubs are in a powerful position to manipulate the NGOs who often do not have enough staff in the field to monitor what is going on. Clubs have even been known to play NGOs off against each other, taking funds from different organizations for the same projects. It is essential that NGOs working in the same areas coordinate more effectively to avoid these kind of incidents. Cooperation with local clubs should be seen as a means to an end, rather than an end in itself. For example, working with clubs need not involve giving long-term employment to club boys, long-term rental of premises belonging to a particular club, placing club boys in key positions implementing the work of the NGO, and so on. If the target group is sex-workers, then the building up of local women's groups and the support of pro-women local leadership is ultimately necessary to re-align power into women's hands. Local men's clubs will only support women up to a point, and only homogeneous groups of women will ultimately be able to take on a role in bringing about long-term changes in their own interest. Internal strategizing to develop clarity of long-term goals is necessary for many of Calcutta's NGOs.

The health and welfare projects that are currently being run by some NGOs only have the potential to effect long-term changes—if indeed this is their objective—only if they see their work as an entry point through which to support local initiatives in order to transfer management to sex-workers and their supporters. Working through clubs that usually have their own political agendas is perhaps only appropriate as a short-term measure, an opportunity through which to nurture and support progressive local leadership, especially among women who feel able to challenge local political interests or who can use the clubs to pursue the agendas of women's groups.

SEX WORKER INITIATIVES

Most welfare interventions do provide basic needs to their beneficiaries, but miss many opportunities for having a greater impact by being uncreative and depending on outsiders to define the needs and work out the details of implementation. The cases of more spontaneous action against exploitation and violence have arisen from the sex-workers themselves, notably in Kalighat and in Sett Bagan.

The Kalighat red-light area has been the site of many struggles that have been resolved in favour of the sex-workers and have resulted in a strong sense of self-reliance and confidence among its residents. In 1972 a group of residents including sex-workers and ex-sex-workers formed a registered organization called Nari Kalyan Samiti. The group was engaged in various social activities in the area such as collecting a group fund from member's contributions for emergencies. For example, this fund was used to buy food during a bad flood when half of the residents had to shift to the local high school because the area was submerged under water. At the time a local politician, a Congress party leader, used to terrorize the sex-workers, and was often drunk, violent and abusive. His behaviour was tolerated for a while but trouble was brewing, and some leaders from the Nari Kalyan Samiti took up the fight against him. Whenever they heard that he was committing atrocities in the area, they would gather as a group and make him leave. He would often fight back and once attacked the local female leader, missing her but seriously injuring another woman who later filed a charge with the police for attempted murder. The man was taken into custody and in the meantime the women gathered 100 to 150 signatures in a petition against him, mostly by sex-workers who were terrified of him. After this man's arrest, members of his gang used to come to the Nari Kalyan Samiti and plead with them. Eventually they agreed with their advocate to drop charges and the man was released, but the women feel that he now respects them for what they did.

Although the Nari Kalyan Samiti successfully stopped the exploitation of Kalighat residents by the local anti-social, the fight brought out political differences within the group, and it split up afterwards. The action against this man did not unite the residents into a strong group, although many individuals gained courage and knew that if they were attacked they would be supported by others. This sense of courage and independence is there to this day. Abahelita Mahila Samiti (AMS) was a new organization formed in 1992 by the same leaders. Four sex-workers are on the committee of AMS, as well as men and women whose mothers are or were sex-workers. One issue that is currently being put forward by some members is reservation for the children of sex-workers for education, hostels and jobs.[9] The group wrote a petition calling for reservation that was signed by 700 to 800 residents of Kalighat, Chetla and Amtala red-light areas, and submitted to ministers in the state government through a local politician in 1993. A conference to discuss the issue was held in June 1994, and several sex-workers from other red-light areas came out in support.

destigmatisation
integration

These demands are a response to the frustrations of belonging to a stigmatized section of society. Advocates of reservation for children of sex-workers draw a parallel between the discrimination they face and the discrimination against the lower castes and scheduled tribes who have successfully bargained for reservations for themselves. It is a very practical solution, as reservations could alleviate the dire poverty of the area and give a real hope for the future if education and jobs were to bring more money and opportunities to the area. It is also a rallying point for creating awareness about the status of the sex-workers and their children, and a way of expressing the demand for positive steps to integrate them into the mainstream.

One question is whether the rest of society is ready to accept their demands. Reservations are already a sensitive political issue, sparking off resentment among other groups who lose out to reserved seats, and it is questionable whether or not this is the best way of improving the status of a community. Clearly linked with this demand is the need for legalization. Reservations would have to be preceded by legal changes that would de-criminalize sex-work totally and have a system of registration. What is striking about this issue is the way that it has sprung up from local residents, and has become a framework within which sex-workers are articulating their demands and raising their voices against their status and the discrimination faced by them and their children.

AMS is currently waiting for full society registration to be granted, after which time they plan to visit clubs in the other Calcutta red-light areas to promote their demand for reservations. The main achievement of AMS so far has been the response to the individual problems of its members and of the residents of Kalighat generally. AMS runs the creche and evening classes for children that are funded by Sanlaap, giving food to the children and taking charge of the day-to-day management. In addition, individual members are known to be social activists who will help with health, legal, and financial problems and in conflicts against landlords who create problems or hoodlums. A lot of support has been given over the years to sex-workers going through difficult times, even in difficult cases involving violence and exploitation. What they have achieved is a strong sense of self-reliance among the Kalighat residents who feel confident and capable of tackling their routine problems. Political groups and NGOs are only called in when some assistance is required, for example, with the police, or for external aid such as financial aid for some women who are sick or in trouble. Most individual cases are otherwise dealt with by the initiative and experience of local residents.

Another initiative took place in Sett Bagan, a small satellite red-light area of Sonagachhi. In the mid-eighties the area was heavily controlled by anti-socials, in particular by one man who extorted money from the residents, abused, humiliated and even raped the sex-workers. Under the leadership of an ex-sex-worker the residents began to organize against the violence and the abuse. Small groups of women would stand on the rooftops at night and raise an alarm when any troublemaker entered the area. Sex-workers along with local women and men would rush to the scene and eject the hooligans. Violence was used on many occasions by both sides—in one incident the leader of the group was badly attacked with an axe, and the police took no action. The residents demonstrated at the police station, demanding the arrest of the anti-social. Finally, he was arrested and imprisoned for a few months.

The sex-workers and other local women formed a group called Mahila Sangha funded by donation boxes set up inside each brothel. This money was used to help out individuals in need, to buy school books for children, clothes for poor members and to contribute to dowries. Later on the group took part in an action to expel the aadhiyas from the area. A small NGO introduced a school and a sewing project at its request. AIIHPH began employing some of the women as peer educators, and the women themselves initiated adult education classes to further their chances of being employed by AIIHPH. In 1993 the Mahila Sangha wrote a leaflet and distributed it at the annual Calcutta Book Fair. A doctor responded to their request and now runs a health centre in the area. In this leaflet the women expressed cynicism and fear of the recent spurt of NGO activity in the red-light areas:

> Nowadays, in response to the AIDS disease, lots and lots of organizations are jumping into the prohibited gully and will not leave without 'serving' us. How they take swipes

at each other—unless you saw it with your own eyes, you would not believe it. One says, 'I will serve you more', while another says, 'No, I will.' We all got very scared. What is it this time? How people change!

At the same time they called for friends and sisters to help them.

Can you help us in any way [to realise this dream]? If you cannot, it does not matter. Still, if you can, at least hinder those who try to obstruct our every move. We will manage to do the rest (Mahila Sangha, 1993).

Later the group and its leadership attained a high public profile and wanted to set up similar groups in all the red-light areas. Many of the AIIHPH peer educators became its members. They aimed for a federation of groups across all the Calcutta red-light areas that could unite to give a unified voice to the demands of the women.[10] Now the initiative has passed on to the Mahila Samanyaya Committes, which seem to have formed the kind of federation envisaged by the Mahila Sangha, which has become less active.

The main priorities of the women in Sett Bagan are now income and child-care. The woman who was their leader then, an ex-sex-worker, set up a children's home in a rural area of West Bengal, and has taken several children whose mothers are sex-workers in either Sonagachhi or Sett Bagan. Her dream of a children's night shelter in the red-light area itself, run entirely by sex-workers, could not be realized because of the difficulty of acquiring space. Instead, she is taking advantage of some land donated to her to go ahead, albeit elsewhere, and will make sure it is run as much as possible by sex-workers themselves.

Interestingly, in Sett Bagan men and non-sex-workers were united with sex-workers in the struggle against the anti-socials, and later they found common needs that were supported and funded by the sex-workers. They successfully organized and managed to throw out their abusers, even though this meant frequent violent confrontations and loss of earnings as the lane was barricaded off. Strong leadership has given the women courage to challenge their exploitation, and the group that came together around this issue has successfully harnessed its energies to bring skills and resources to Sett Bagan.

Both Abahelita Mahila Samiti and Mahila Sangha have sprung up from local leadership and have challenged abusive anti-socials. They have been strongly led by local women who have gained the respect of the residents by engaging in violent confrontations for a social cause. They have then gone on to interact with NGOs and the government (both are involved in the AIIHPH STD/HIV Project), taking advantage of the funds that are coming into the red-light areas and being involved in their distribution. One leader has been drawn into party politics and is now a Congress party activist. The other leader is less involved with politics but has a strong sense of fighting for a cause, for the rights of sex-worker's from an activist's perspective.

What remains to be seen is to what extent these local leaders and the groups they formed will be co-opted by the state and the NGOs to implement projects and pursue the agendas of outsiders. Group members are often dependent on their leaders. The position of these leaders is unwittingly reinforced by outsiders who channel funds through them, and even ask them to select local people for jobs when employing local staff. Individual sex-workers are not being organized as a group through these leaders and are still not in a position to voice their own personal needs that may differ from those of their leaders. This encourages concentration of power into the hands of the leaders and is not accompanied by group-strengthening activities. When this occurs it is unlikely that the groups will be strengthened over time, and so a lot depends on the leaders remaining pro-women and not themselves being co-opted by the system or corrupted by power. NGO and state interventions are dependent on these local groups and therefore on their leaders, just as they are dependent on the men's clubs in other areas. If there is an absence of strong group feeling among the members of both women's groups, they are actually quite vulnerable to becoming passive beneficiaries of projects defined and managed by outsiders.

We are a long way from the ideal that sex-workers will come together into well-organized groups. So much is at stake, and so many vested interests would be threatened. Perhaps all we can hope for in the immediate future is that the leaders who have the interests of the women at heart continue to support the rights of the sex-workers, that they manage to rise above political party agendas, co-optation and corruption. In the meantime, much would be gained if the outsiders who go to work in the red-light areas work more closely with the local groups as partners and decision-makers, rather than as implementing agents of their projects. Because partnerships between local groups and outsider organizations would then become more equal, it would help to make projects more effective and more need-based. The NGOs working with the same groups need to co-ordinate their efforts and think more strategically about the long-term impact of their work. If NGOs, representatives of government programmes, and the sex-worker groups could agree on some common objectives for meeting both the practical and the long-term strategic needs of the sex-workers, they could at least co-ordinate their efforts, and perhaps work together to share a common platform.

NOTES

1. Dr. Anup Roy and Linda Chakraborty of Development Dialogue, personal communication, 1996.
2. Child in Need Institute, a sister organization of CINI (ASHA).
3. Sulagna Roy, project officer, CINI (ASHA), personal communication, 1996.
4. Dr. R. C. Biswas, Director, CRS, personal communication, 1996.
5. Mrs. Kusum Gupta, secretary, Jabala, personal communication, 1996.
6. Mallika Jalan, director, and Paramita Roy, research and planning, of CCC, personal communication, 1996.
7. Dr. S. Jana, project director of AIIHPH STDs/HIV Programme, personal communication, 1996.
8. The child-to-child approach was evolved within health education, and involves training children with health knowledge that they share with other children.
9. Policy akin to affirmative action geared to selected castes and groups in India. Since the benefits are considerabnle, many disadvantages groups lobby for inclusion.
10. Dr. Joseph Chandy runs a medical clinic; Catrin Evans is carrying out research as an anthropologist at Sett Bagan; personal communication, 1996.

CHAPTER 9

Ways Forward

'Morality has two genders.'—UN/ESCAP

MANY SEX-WORKERS ARE simply survivors of marriage and family break-ups. Their stories even before joining the sex industry are a shameful record of human rights' abuse. Their entry into the sex trade is often aided by agents or known people who seek personal gain. Once they join the industry they are surrounded by men and women who profit from their work. The chukri system is the most direct form of exploitation where the sex-workers are like bonded labourers. The aadhiya system is also exploitative as an inflated proportion of the money earned, instead of a fixed rent, is handed over to the mashis. In certain areas, the police regularly take their cut for allowing businesses to flourish, not just by turning a blind eye but by actively collaborating to ensure money flows in their direction. The extent of the collaboration of the police with the sex industry is an indictment of society and reveals a complete lack of understanding of the spirit of the 'tolerance' laws.

After paying their compulsory handouts, after supporting children and their families back in the villages or home towns, the money left to the sex-worker drains away to a host of other people. Moneylenders take their share of interest on loans, plus any extras that can be cheated from non-literate customers. Traders come door to door offering clothes, jewellery, and food on credit that when finally paid off inflates the cost of the items. Some babus cheat, exploit and abuse their mistresses. Large amounts of money go on health-care as the work and lifestyle causes ill-health and yet demands quick treatment so that the flow of clients is not interrupted. The position of the state does not help as it passes and implements laws with a hypocrisy befitting a patriarchal and corrupt institution. From politicians to court clerks, functionaries of the state have time and again lined their pockets with money from the sex trade. Legal clauses that criminalize sex-workers have been used to extract money, intimidate and even gain free sex from sex-workers. Sex-workers are viewed by law-makers and the state alike as fallen women who have no right to justice, to freedom from violence or rape, who have lost their right to be a part of this society that has created them.

The economic base of the industry is far greater than the gains to the sex-workers would suggest. As in most industries, the smallest rewards go to the primary workers, and yet in this trade the financial exploitation of these workers is exacerbated, aided by the ambiguous legal status of the sex industry. In addition, it is the workers and not the organizers of the trade who feel the impact of the stigmatization and isolation. The hardships caused by loss of 'honour', the health risks, exposure to violence, police harassment, effects on children and old age insecurity are far from being compensated by financial rewards.

Despite the hardships, many women are survivors. Their strength lies in their ability to cope with the hardships in addition to their everyday workload. Working as heads of households, sex-workers have to balance many roles—being the main breadwinner, managing the household, and taking responsibility for raising children. Their relationships with their clients are diverse, and many women aim to find fixed clients who can pay regular monthly sums, and with whom they may have the chance of a relationship beyond simply commercial sex. Some fixed clients become live-in partners, maintaining their mistresses as well as their own families elsewhere, moving between two households. Fluidity and flexibility in relationships is the norm. As the involvement of married clients shows, this flexibility is not only isolated to the red-light areas but exists in the rest of society where men are able to have multiple sexual partners and still be accepted in public life.

The histories and lifestyles of women in the sex trade, as well as the needs of their clients, are potent examples revealing that stability and security within families are myths. Stories of bigamy, desertion, divorce, violence, sexual abuse, child marriage, bereavement, followed closely by destitution, are commonplace. The women's life stories reveal tragedies that speak volumes about the vulnerability of women living in poverty in Indian society, the conflicts within families when faced with crises or violations of traditional norms, especially with regard to sexual behaviour. Abuse against women within the family is linked to their vulnerability because their tolerance is expected, and indeed they are likely to accept it because their security cannot be guaranteed outside the family. Many women who do venture out of dysfunctional families to earn an independent living find that neither they nor society are adequately equipped for this role. Yet the reality is that many women do have to survive independently of their husbands and families. Given limited job opportunities, inappropriate skills for the labour market, and the commodification of women, joining the sex trade is an obvious coping strategy, very often a survival strategy. Ironically, the same hypocratical family values that have pushed these women in the outside world to fend for themselves are perpetuated in the profession they practise. Society upholds its hypocritical values by denying commercial sex-workers legal rights, a voice against police harassment, possibilities of alternative employment, or secure futures for their children.

Women's sexuality is seen to be central to their honour and their acceptance as brides and wives, while men's honour is tied to their conduct in public life. New brides must be virgins, while grooms can be sexually experienced. Sexual double standards persist within marriage where female infidelity is an outrage and male infidelity merely an embarrassment. It is time for us to face up to this hypocrisy and examine its consequences. To cater to men's desire for self-gratification, a whole under-class of women has been created, women who are denied their basic human rights. Sex-workers have a right to dignity and well-being. Striving for this goes beyond welfare and involves a struggle for rights.

To end on a positive note, we will highlight some possible future interventions that we feel would help to address both the short-term and long-term needs of the sex-workers. The following suggestions are particularly important for an effective and gender-sensitive approach in working for sex-workers' rights:

(*i*) Support existing local initiatives and promote networking and coordination between different sex-worker groups, locally and nationally.

(*ii*) Improve coordination between NGOs, and enhance dialogue and networking between NGOs and the government.

(*iii*) Support or establish centres in red-light areas that can offer legal advice, counselling and crisis-intervention to sex-workers, staffed by local residents, assisted by local volunteers.

(*iv*) Equip red-light areas with child-care facilities, ideally night-shelters, employing and/or being managed by elderly former sex-workers and ensuring that timings are suited to the working hours of the mothers.

(*v*) Open short-stay shelter homes and refuges for girls and women victims of violence and sexual abuse.

(*vi*) Broaden the scope of HIV-related projects away from purely epidemiological goals to broader social objectives, such as strengthening sex-workers' negotiating powers and building up local leadership.

(*vii*) More research and action on sex-workers' own prioritized health problems.

(*viii*) Promote savings and credit schemes as a group activity to improve women's economic situation and release them from indebtedness to moneylenders. Credit groups can also be an excellent means of building group capacity and fostering group identity.

(*ix*) Reach out to male sex-workers and floating sex-workers who are even more isolated than the female sex-workers who live in red-light areas. See clients as an important target group for STD interventions, and reach clients through their workplace, village men's groups, hostels, mainstream media, social centres, and so on.

(*x*) Challenge the division of labour by gender that confines and limits women's options in the labour market. Employment-generation schemes must go beyond sex stereotypes, and women should be trained in marketable skills that will enable them to be independent.

(*xi*) Lobby for more women police officers, particularly in stations near red-light areas.

(*xii*) Train and sensitize the police regarding the laws on the sex trade. Lobby for severe penalties and action against state representatives who harass sex-workers, extort money, make deals with traffickers and collaborate with the organizers of the sex trade. Sensitize the police to the issues relating to crimes against women, and to the rights of sex-workers to protection from the law.

(*xiii*) Lobby for review of the laws on prostitution, strongly involving sex-workers in the debate. Reduce police powers to harass sex-workers.

(*xiv*) Lobby for better enforcement of laws against trafficking, for tightening up border control between Nepal and Bangladesh, and for communication and coordination between the relevant authorities and NGOs in sending and receiving countries.

(*xv*) Sensitize government and NGO staff working in the red-light areas to gender issues relating to and arising from the sex trade, and raise awareness of the link between the sex trade, its artificial isolation and patriarchy. This can be done through gender training, evaluation of existing interventions and media from a gender perspective, and through giving sex-workers a platform for airing their own views and experiences.

(*xvi*) Lobby against representations in the media that portray women as sex objects and convey messages about women as commodities to be purchased and possessed.

(*xvii*) More dialogue and cooperation between women's rights activists and sex-workers is needed. Sex-workers could form links with a movement that challenges women being judged by their sexuality, women having limited options for economic independence, and so on. In turn, the women's movement in India could be strengthened by lobbying for the rights of sex-workers as women who have a right to society's support and respect.

APPENDICES

I. MALE COMMERCIAL SEX-WORKERS IN CALCUTTA

Male commercial sex-workers cater to male clients in many areas of Calcutta. Traditionally *malish wallahs* (masseurs) and *hijras* (eunuchs)[1] provide commercial sex to men along with other non-sexual services. Unfortunately, we have very little information about either of these groups. Here we will look very briefly at men who are part of the cruising network of 'men who have sex with men' for pleasure, and who make extra income by charging their partners money. Calcutta has many areas where men who have sex with men cruise for sexual partners, and the network has eight major centres where there are concentrations of male sex-workers.

The network arose to meet the needs of 'gay' men, 'gay' being used rather imprecisely in this context as many members also have sex with women, are married, and do not have a gay identity. For example, many of the men have sex with other men because they want sexual release and men happen to be more easily accessible than women. These men may leave the gay network once they are married. Network members usually expect and want a family and a wife, and view sex with a wife as a duty even if they prefer sex with men. Whether the men have sex with same- or different-sex partners is flexible : it is not unusual for male sex-workers to be clients of female sex-workers, and for the clients of male sex-workers to pay for sex also with women.

Most male sex-workers do not begin working for commercial reasons, but after some time realize that others are engaging in the same activities for commercial gain, and begin charging some of their clients. It is usually the financially needy who end up working commercially. If they like one of their clients they may stop taking money from him when they have sex. These sex-workers see their identity as closer to the female sex-workers than to hijras or malish wallahs.

As with female sex-workers, men may have several fixed clients whom they refer to as their babus, or may have serially monogamous relationships, feeling that they are faithful to one person mentally even though they continue to have sex with others. Male sex-workers work in the cruising centres, generally in parks, railway stations, public toilets, and so on. Some clients will pay for a hotel room. The charges vary according to the kinds of risk faced by the sex-workers and the privacy of the space that determines the explicitness of the sexual act. Also, the richer the client, the higher the rate charged. Most of the sex-workers have other paid work, often informal and irregular, and their income is supplemented by their commercial sex-work. Male sex-workers are organized into informal social groups, each with their own leader who takes care of finances, resolves conflicts and handles the police. Group members pool their incomes each day. Some is spent on common activities and on payments to the police, while the group leader shares out the rest among the members. The groups are not organized primarily around the commercial aspect but are first and foremost social groups where men can express their alternative identities, often effeminate or with hijra language and mannerisms.

The risks are high. They face verbal and physical violence from the police, clients, anti-socials or hoodlums, and pimps of female sex-workers. The police regularly extort money from male sex-workers. This is usually done informally, but occasionally the men are taken to the police station and they have to pay anything up to four or five hundred rupees. Meetings with clients can turn violent if clients refuse to pay. Anti-socials and political hoodlums threaten the men. Pimps of female sex-workers and the female sex-workers themselves are in competition with the male sex-workers who provide similar sexual services (masturbation, oral sex and anal sex). A lot of the violence that male sex-workers face is related to this competition for clients and space. Because of the violent nature of the work, the culture of the network is very aggresive and several of the men claim to have learnt karate. Publicly they put on a very aggressive hijra act. They also have their own language, a mixture of terms and accents used by hijras and female sex-workers, through which communication is private and therefore safer.

Health is a major problem and most male sex-workers know about STDs through experience. They have no access to free or subsidized condoms, and no privacy or space to use them. They are treated badly by the staff of hospitals and clinics.

Male sex-workers are even more of an invisible group than female sex-workers. Their isolation is extreme as they, like female floating sex-workers, do not live in communities but return to families at the end of each day. Traditionally homosexual sex is shrouded in silence, not openly condemned but tolerated provided that men who have sex with men (and women who have sex with women) do so in silence and lead an outwardly heterosexual life.

Male commercial sex-workers, their wives and their clients are at risk from HIV/AIDS, yet at present no HIV/AIDS interventions reach them. A NGO intervention in the pipeline is the Naz Foundation that is starting a male sexual health project for male sex-workers in Calcutta. The project will work through the existing informal network and will give sexual health training to network members.[2]

NOTES

1. The term *hijra* describes a community of hermaphrodites, eunuchs and men who have an alternative sexuality. They play a special role in Indian society because they give their blessings at births and marriages and are always propitiated with gifts and money since it is believed that not doing so will bring bad luck. They are devotees of the Goddess Bahuchara Mata.
2. Debanuj Das Gupta, co-ordinator, Naz Foundation (India) Project, personal communication, 1996.

II. SOME LAWS AND VERDICTS RELEVANT TO SEX-WORKERS

1992 Supreme Court ruling that children of sex-workers are not required to give father's name for school admission. West Bengal Commission for Women Act passed. Autonomous investigative body with powers of a civil court

1990 Juvenile Welfare Boards set up in West Bengal. National Commission on Women Act passed to monitor legislation and tighten laws.

1990 Women awaiting trial (except for major offences) no longer kept in jails.

1986 Immoral Traffic in Persons (Prevention) Act (PITA) passed (amendment to SITA, 1956)
Central Juvenile Justice Act replaces 22 state acts. Children no longer kept in jails. Juvenile Courts to be established; Child Labour (Prohibition and Regulation) Act passed.

1984 Dedication Prevention Act bans system of dedicating devadasis or temple dancers to temples.

1976 Bonded Labour (Abolition) Act passed.

1972 India's first all-women police station set up in Kerala.

1956 Suppression of Immoral Traffic Act (SITA) passed.

1950 India signatory to UN Conference Declaration for the Suppression of Traffic in Women and Girls.

1933 Bengal Suppression of Immoral Traffic Act passed.

1923 Calcutta Suppression of Immoral Traffic Bill introduced to suppress brothels, trafficking and soliciting.

1907 East Bengal and Assam Disorderly Houses Act passed for suppression of brothels.

1886 Cantonment Acts for regulation of prostitutes and British soldiers.

1883 Contagious Diseases Act suspended as seen as state participation in the 'immoral' sex industry.

1868 Contagious Diseases Act applies in all major cities in India.

1866 Calcutta Police Act prohibits use of rooms or houses for sex-work.

1864 Contagious Diseases Act passed in Britain, also applies to India, requires sex-workers to be registered and examined weekly for sexually transmitted diseases.

1860 Indian Penal Code introduced, with sections covering procuring and trafficking of women.

III. ADDRESSES OF SELECTED ORGANIZATIONS

The work of the following organizations has been discussed in Chapter 8. These are just a sample of some of them. They can be contacted at the following addresses:

ALL-INDIA INSTITUTE OF HYGIENE
   AND PUBLIC HEALTH
STD/HIV Intervention Programme
110 Chittaranjan Avenue
Calcutta 700 073

BHORUKA PUBLIC WELFARE TRUST
63, Rafi Ahmed Kidwai Road,
Calcutta 700 016

CENTRE FOR CONTEMPORARY
   COMMUNICATION
6/7A A.J.C. Bose Road
Calcutta 700 017

CINI (ASHA)
Amader Bari
63 Rafi Ahmed Kidwai Road
Calcutta 700 016

CATHEDRAL RELIEF SERVICE
St Paul's Cathedral
Calcutta 700 020

JABALA
6A Outram Street
Calcutta 700 017

NAZ FOUNDATION (INDIA) TRUST
Calcutta Project
468A, Block-K New Alipore
Calcutta 700 053

SANLAAP
171A Rashbehari Avenue
Calcutta 700 029

Bibliography

AIDS Bhedhav Virodhi Andolan (ABVA). 1990. 'Women and AIDS: Denial and Blame: A Citizen's Report.' New Delhi: ABVA.

All Bengal Women's Union. 1988. Survey of Prostitution in Calcutta for UNIFEM/UNDP. Calcutta: ABWU.

Ain O Salish Kendro. 1994. 'Situation Report: Trafficking of Women in Bangladesh.' Paper presented at The International Workshop on Migration and Traffic in Women, Thailand.

All-India Institute of Hygiene and Public Health (AIIH&PH). 1993. 'Sexual Behaviour, Knowledge and Attitude Towards STD/HIV among Commercial Sex-Workers in Calcutta.' Paper presented at Workshop on Sexual Aspects of AIDS/STD Prevention in India, Tata Institute of Social Sciences, Bombay.

—. 1996. Namaskar (newsletter) of the Project Team, STD/HIV Intervention Programme. Edited by S. Singh (January).

Chakraborty, S. 1989. 'Special Report to Dhaka: Report to Bangladeshi High Commission on Trafficking of Women.' Amrita Bazar Patrika.

Chatterjee, Ratnabali. 1992. 'The Queen's Daughters: Prostitutes as an Outcaste Group in Colonial India.' Paper presented at Chr. Michelsen Institute, Fantoft, Norway.

Child in Need Institute. 1992. 'Interim Report on Abuse of Children as part of Commercialised Vice.' Calcutta: CINI.

—'A Pilot Study of the Sexual Practices of the Sex-Workers in a Red-Light Area of Calcutta.' 1993. Paper presented at Workshop on Sexual Aspects of AIDS/STD Prevention in India, Tata Institute of Social Sciences, Bombay.

D'Cunha, J. 1991. *The Legalization of Prostitution*. Bangalore: Word-makers.

Das, R., and R. Chopra. 1990. 'Prostitution: How to Deal with It?' *Social Welfare* (Central Social Welfare Board) (June).

Das Gupta, A. 1990. 'Causes of Prostitution and Methods of Prevention.' *Social Welfare* (Central Social Welfare Board) (June).

Das Gupta, S., M. Ghosh, and A. Das Gupta. 1989-1990. 'Revati: A Survey. *Samya Shakti* 4 & 5: 232-43.

Evans, C. 1995. 'Ethnographic Study of Sexual Health and Related Health-Seeking Behaviour among Commercial Sex Workers and Poor Women in a Northern Calcutta Slum.' Paper presented at London School of Hygiene and Tropical Medicine.

Garcia-Moreno, C. 1991. 'AIDS: Women Are Not Just Transmitters.' in *Changing Perceptions*, edited by T. Wallace and C. March. Oxford: Oxfam.

Haksar, N. 1992. *Demystification of Law for Women*. New Delhi: Lancer Press.

Institute for Psychological and Educational Research (IPER). 1990. 'Child Exploitation and Abuse: A Global Phenomenon.' Report of the First Asian Conference on Child Exploitation and Abuse, Calcutta. Calcutta 1990.

Government of India, Ministry of Home Affairs. 1989. 'Crime in India.' National Crime Records Bureau. New Delhi.

Joarder, B. 1984. *Prostitution in Modern and Historical Perspectives*. New Delhi: Inter-India.

—. 1985. *Prostitution in Nineteenth-Century and Early Twentieth-Century Calcutta*. New Delhi: Inter-India.

Jyoti, B. C., and M. Poudel. 1994. 'Trafficking of Women in Nepal: An Overview.' Paper presented at The International Workshop on Migration and Traffic in Women', Thailand.

McLeod, E. 1985. *Women Working: Prostitution Now*. London: Croom Helm.

Mahila Sangha. 1993. '*Barbonita Bolchi.*' (Speaking about Ourselves) Leaflet translated by Joseph Chandy.

Menon, R. 1992. 'Sexual Abuse of Children—Hidden Peril.' *India Today* (31 October).

Pai Patkar, P. 1990. 'Children of Prostitutes: A Perspective.' *Social Welfare* (Central Social Welfare Board) (June).

Rao, A. R. 1990. 'The Health Status of the Prostitutes and Their Children.' *Social Welfare* (Central Social Welfare Board) (June).

Rozario, R. 1988. *Trafficking in Women and Children in India*. New Delhi: Uppal Publishing House.

Sancho, N. 1994. 'Trafficking in Women as Human Rights Violations' AWHRC, Philippines.' Paper presented on behalf of AWHRC at The International Workshop on Migration and Traffic in Women, Thailand.

Sanlaap. 1994. 'Survey Results'.

Singh, S. 1995. 'Three-Year Stint at Sonagachhi: An Exposition.' Paper presented at AIIHPH, Calcutta.

Sinha, I. 1992. 'Use Me No More.' Calcuta: Sanlaap.

Society for Research on Haemotology and Blood Transfusion. 1993. 'A Study on Sexual Behaviour Patterns of Truck Drivers and Helpers.' Paper presented at Workshop on Sexual Aspects of AIDS/STD Prevention in India, Tata Institute of Social Sciences, Bombay.

Standing, H. 1991. *Dependence and Autonomy: Women's Employment and the Family in Calcutta.* London: Routledge.

UN/ESCAP. 1986. 'Virtue, Order, Health and Money: Towards a Comprehensive Perspective on Female Prostitution in Asia.' Bangkok.

UNICEF. 1990. 'Children and Women in India: A Situational Analysis.' New Delhi. 1992

Van der Vleuten, N. 1994. 'Survey on "Traffic in Women" Policies and Policy-Research in an International Context.' (VENA Working Paper 91/1) Paper presented at The International Workshop on Migration and Traffic in Women, Thailand.

INDEX